From the Hearts of Mums

Stories of love
and inclusion
in the world of
Down syndrome

Julie Fisher

First published by Ultimate World Publishing 2023
Copyright © 2023 Julie Fisher

ISBN

Paperback: 978-1-922982-08-7
Ebook: 978-1-922982-09-4

Julie Fisher has asserted her rights under the Copyright, Designs and Patents Act 1988 to be identified as the author of this work. The information in this book is based on the author's experiences and opinions. The publisher specifically disclaims responsibility for any adverse consequences which may result from use of the information contained herein. Permission to use information has been sought by the author. Any breaches will be rectified in further editions of the book.

All rights reserved. No part of this publication may be reproduced, stored in or introduced into a retrieval system, or transmitted in any form, or by any means (electronic, mechanical, photocopying, recording or otherwise) without the prior written permission of the author. Any person who does any unauthorised act in relation to this publication may be liable to criminal prosecution and civil claims for damages. Enquiries should be made through the publisher.

Cover design: Alexis Schnitger Design
Layout and typesetting: Ultimate World Publishing
Editor: Marinda Wilkinson

Ultimate World Publishing
Diamond Creek,
Victoria Australia 3089
www.writeabook.com.au

Praise for Julie's Work

Can you imagine a world where everybody truly accepted one another? This is just the start of that conversation for some, and the continued fight for others like Julie and Darcy. Thank you so much to the both of you for sharing your story and lived experience when it comes to this massively important topic. I know firsthand that it hasn't been easy at times, but I also know that it's been because of those challenges that you continue to advocate for real acceptance and inclusion. This book is an important step in the right direction, and I genuinely can't wait for people to start reading.

KRISTIAN SERAINIDIS
Founder, Project Kick It

The Unexpected Journey is a relatable, emotive and powerful story shared through the lived experience of a courageous mother and woman. Julie's ability to capture and articulate Darcy and her family's journey will resonate with all parents, as well as provide a few laughs and tears along the way. Every individual brings diverse abilities and attributes which makes our world a better place and Julie expresses this beautifully throughout her writing. In her second book, Julie shares personal stories of the profound impact of inclusion, and why it is critically important as a society we provide equal access to opportunities and resources for people who might otherwise be excluded or marginalised. Congratulations Julie on sharing your story which has many more exciting chapters to come!

DAN PAYNE
CEO, Down Syndrome Victoria

Contents

Dedication	ix
Thank You	xi
Introduction	1
LUCAS AND KERRY-ANN	3
IZZY AND SARAH	21
LINCOLN AND STEPHANIE	45
CASSIE AND ELLEN	67
EVAN AND STACEY	83
DARCY AND JULIE	95
ERIN AND DIANE	115
SAXON AND NARELLE	139
AMY AND TINA	153
JOEL AND ISOBEL	169
NINO AND SHARON	189
COURTNEY AND DI	211
DOUG AND BONNIE	227
Afterword	253
About The Author	255
About The Designer	259
Offers	263
Speaker Bio	265

*Parenthood is about raising and
celebrating the child you have, not
the child you thought you'd have. It's
about understanding your child is
exactly the person they are supposed
to be. And, if you're lucky, they might
be the teacher who turns you into the
person you are supposed to be.*

Joan Ryan, The Water Giver

*And I'd choose you,
in a hundred lifetimes, in a hundred worlds,
in any version of reality, I'd find
you and I'd choose you.*

Kiersten White, The Chaos of Stars

Dedication

To all our beautiful babies and people we care for.
All our stories are different, but we travel the same road.
Sharing with love.

Thank You

I would like to extend a huge thank you to all the beautiful ladies who have contributed to this book, sharing stories of life with their loved ones.

Some are friends from Australia, and some are new friends from the United Kingdom and the United States who I met remotely during lockdowns in Covid times. I'm so very grateful to them all for their valuable contributions.

So, thank you to …

Kerry-Ann Bellamy
Sarah Mayes
Stephanie Rodden
Ellen Huggins
Stacey Byrne
Diane Compton
Narelle Wilson
Tina Naughton

From the Hearts of Mums

Isobel Serle-Flannery
Sharon Genua
Di Sermon
Bonnie Clayton-Daugherty

As you read their stories, you will notice some of their experiences are very different. This is partly because of where they live. It is also because every family has a different story.

From country to country, and family to family, things can vary greatly, although the common thread throughout this book is that all the stories centre around our loved ones who live with Down syndrome.

When our loved ones joined our families, they introduced us to the world of disability and the Down syndrome community. Even though we are all travelling along the same road, we may end up in different lanes with different stories to tell.

There is also something very similar between all our loved ones and I wonder, as you read the pages in this book, if you can see what it is. I think it's beautiful that they share this wonderful warm emotion.

Inclusion and acceptance is what we want to see for our loved ones. We all would love to see a world where they are recognised for who they are and given an opportunity to live their best life no matter what.

GIVE PEOPLE A CHANCE AND WATCH THEM SHINE
Julie Fisher

Introduction

Since the publication of my previous books, *The Unexpected Journey* and *The Magic of Inclusion* I have received many comments from people who enjoyed reading about our journey and learning how important it is for our son Darcy to be treated as any other person would like to be treated.

Many also expressed how they didn't realise that inclusion and acceptance, even though things are much better than many years ago, is still often lacking. People are genuinely surprised when I share stories of what we and our friends have experienced and have had to deal with from people.

The feedback from my books is overwhelmingly one of gratitude for sharing and providing an insight into our world. Many people say they really enjoy hearing about the world we live in and getting to know our son Darcy a little more.

Sharing our story gives an insight into our experiences, however, everyone's stories are different. I decided it was important to also share the stories of other families, and the idea for this book was born.

Inside, you will hear from 13 families, and you will see their stories are different from ours, even though we all travel along the same road. You will also see that each and every one of us have the same wants for our loved ones.

We want them to be accepted for who they are. We want them to have the opportunity to shine and try all the things in life they would like to try. We want them to be part of all the things that most of us take for granted.

Our children and those we care for deserve to live life as everyone else does, even though there may be some obstacles and challenges in the way. Everyone deserves to feel comfortable in whatever it is they choose to do.

You will see that all of the families in this book have had to advocate for their loved ones in many different ways and you will notice how experiences can vary depending on where they live.

I am honoured these beautiful families have shared their journeys with me in this book.

I hope you enjoy hearing their stories from all over the world as much as I did.

LUCAS AND KERRY-ANN
Sutton-in-Ashfield, Nottinghamshire, England

Lucas, Aged 2 Years

Lucas is our third child and he arrived in the world to join our family six days after our due date. I was monitored closely for that last week because I was losing fluid and we weren't sure where it was coming from. Thankfully everything went well and Lucas was born without any complications.

It was a very quick labour, just 45 minutes, but it was hard! Seeing his beautiful face definitely made it worthwhile. We couldn't be happier to welcome our last bundle of joy. Our family was now complete.

We did not receive the diagnosis of Down syndrome (Trisomy 21) when Lucas was first born. The official diagnosis would not come until he was 10 days old.

We spent a couple of nights in the hospital as his temperature was not regulating, and the staff were basically doing everything they could to regulate his temperature before we went home. This seemed to be the focus after he was born rather than anything else.

Before we went home and they came to do the initial checks, there was mention made about the epicanthal folds on his eyes, but it was dismissed as the doctor said that it can be normal. The discussion never went any further from that point. I didn't know any different and just accepted it for what he said.

He was the doctor and I guess I thought, if the doctor says it's fine, then it's fine. Mind you, I did go to Google and when I typed that in, the first thing that popped up was Down syndrome. I still didn't really think twice about it.

The night Lucas was born we put photos on social media announcing his arrival, and one of Scott's friends sent him a message saying, 'I'm sorry that he has Down syndrome.' We were completely oblivious and didn't really pick up on it, but we did think it was strange that he made that comment. I don't think we thought too much about it because none of the medical professionals had mentioned Down syndrome and we just dismissed the comment. He was, after all, just born and all squishy.

We went home after a two-night stay in the hospital and when Robyn and Harry met their new little brother, they were absolutely besotted with him. They just adored him and wouldn't leave him alone. It was lovely to see them all together.

Robyn was instantly like a second little mummy to Lucas and completely nurtured him whereas Harry initially said he didn't like him which made us laugh. It didn't take long for him to warm up and completely love him. Seeing the three of them just filled me with pride and love. I got a sense that they would all be best friends as well as siblings.

Harry was very curious when it came to breastfeeding and I remember a time when he asked me if it was coming from my belly. My reply, as I've always felt giving an honest answer to a question asked is the best approach, was telling him no, and explaining he is sucking from mummy's boobie.

Harry then proceeded to lift up his top and point to his own chest and chase Robyn around the living room saying, 'Robyn drink my milk!' Oh my goodness, we all laughed so hard we cried!

We spent the next couple of days at home, as it was during lockdown in 2020 and we couldn't go anywhere. It was at the time where you were only allowed to go out for one hour exercise, like a walk. Apart from that and going to the supermarket, we weren't allowed to go anywhere else.

We took the opportunity to go for a walk around the block because it was a beautiful day and we had been in hospital and indoors since he was born. It was lovely to get outside in some fresh air, but Lucas spent the whole time crying. We couldn't work out what was wrong but tried to soothe him and kept on with the walk.

By the time we got back home, he had become really quiet and had actually started to turn blue around his nose and around his mouth. It was very frightening, and we rang the midwife because we were told if there were any problems to call her.

I was breastfeeding at the time as well and she said it could be normal for a breastfed baby and not to worry. I did think it was strange that she said that, but again trusted what she said. She asked me to wait on the line a minute and then came back and told me to call 111 to be on the safe side.

The call to 111 was made and we gave them all the details of what was happening. They didn't like the sound of what we told them and sent an ambulance straight out. When they arrived, they took one look at Lucas and basically threw him in the back of the ambulance with me. We were blue lighted straight to the resuscitation unit.

My head was spinning. What was happening? It was very frightening, and I was so worried about our little boy.

I wasn't thinking clearly at this point because everything was going so fast. My emotions were all over the place and I was feeling very confused. I just stood out of the way holding his change bag and the clothes they had taken off him while watching them give him oxygen and try to rouse him to get a response.

Lucas was number one priority at this point, and I let them do their job by not getting too close. Don't get me wrong I was devasted and all I wanted to do was hold my boy, but crying hysterically and getting in the way would not have done any good. The focus needed to be on Lucas.

They started doing some tests that showed he had low blood sugar. They weren't happy with what was happening with him because he wasn't feeding, and he was not responding well.

When we arrived at the hospital, they took him straight into resuscitation, and that's when they also started to pick up on his features. It was funny because I remember when they did an X-ray of his chest, they said 'Do you know his heart is slightly enlarged?' Having a little bit of information on Down syndrome myself, I knew this was one of the markers for Down syndrome.

When they told me about his heart, the first thing I asked was, 'Does he have Down syndrome?' I was told, yes, he does show prominent features. This is when they also asked me if we knew about genetic testing.

They didn't seem concerned that the diagnosis had been missed when he was born, or at least they didn't show it. They certainly didn't say to me that it was concerning it had been missed.

I look back at our first pictures now and kick myself, it's so obvious that the features are there in his little face, the almond shaped eyes, the tongue sticking out, the eye folds.

It makes me angry still to this day that it was missed because if it was picked up on, he could have had all the necessary checks done and it's absolutely a possibility that what happened may well have not.

So much was going on, it was hard to take it all in and at the same time they thought it was possible that he was unresponsive because he had an infection. He ended up on five different antibiotics immediately and then they started with heart and MRI scans.

After days of monitoring and multiple scans, the doctors concluded that he had suffered a stroke when he was first admitted into the hospital.

This is where my breakdown came. Flood gates opened, and I remember looking at the doctor after he had finished talking to me and asking him, 'Please can we go home, I just want to go home?' I say asked, but begged would be a better word.

I was desperate to be with my family as it had been just me and Lucas at the hospital thanks to Covid restrictions not allowing visits. Not even Scott could come and see us while we were there.

After my question, that wonderful man said yes! We got to go home that same day. I was so relieved, scared and confused. But we were going home!

All his markers for infection had come back clear and he was able to come off all the antibiotics. They managed his breathing and regulated his oxygen with support. When he reached the point where he didn't need the support of oxygen, we were able to go and stay home. He had spent a total of six days in hospital.

Lucas, Aged 2 Years

All of the medical issues we were dealing with at that point were more shocking than the Down syndrome diagnosis. We were feeling very devastated by everything that was happening rather than the diagnosis they gave us.

We were still waiting on the genetic testing results, and it was Easter weekend which meant it took longer. We were settled for the weekend and enjoying some time together in the garden when the phone call came confirming the diagnosis of Down syndrome or Trisomy 21 as they said.

They were really positive about it on the phone and there was no negativity at all. They said he's tested positive for Trisomy 21, and we want to get you in so we can talk about everything and let you know what happens next and in the future. They were brilliant and had us come in the very next day.

We sat for a long time and just chatted while they gave us information, booklets and leaflets for support and education. They did tell us not to Google it because we wouldn't get anything positive out of what we saw online.

We received congratulations from everyone, and it was a really positive experience for us. I know a lot of people experience negativity, hearing comments like 'Oh, I'm sorry he's got Down syndrome', or being given advice toward termination in pregnancy, but we've never experienced that at all. It's been really good and has been very positive right from the start.

That really helped us because we did still go through the emotions of feeling sad and going through a grieving process. But I think that's because what we had been expecting hadn't happened and we just needed to get our heads around it.

But friends and family have also always been so supportive, and their attitude has always been that it doesn't matter, it's fine and it's okay. We have felt fully supported right from the moment Lucas was born which has been great.

The first few months we couldn't have visitors because of Covid restrictions but in a sense, it gave us time to process, research and prepare, in our own little bubble.

Family were fantastic bringing us what we needed and just by being besotted with him it made us feel, I guess, in a way normal. Like we had just had a baby and it was all exciting and not doom and gloom.

A lot of sadness enveloped us at this time but seeing people, family and friends just treat this as a wonderful time helped that process.

Lucas has a beautiful relationship with his aunties, uncles and cousins who all love to make him laugh and smother him in snuggles and kisses.

Same with all his grandparents, they love to see him, just as they do Robyn and Harry. Lucas is never treated any differently to his siblings and they all get the same love and affection from all family members, and I just love that.

Some of the supports we were linked up to from the hospital were the Down Syndrome Association, Positive About Down Syndrome, and a big one in our area that we linked up with is Nottinghamshire Down Syndrome Support Group. We were in contact with all of those support networks as soon as we received Lucas's diagnosis.

Lucas, Aged 2 Years

We were told if you want to get good information, these are the places to get it from. There will be other families there as well for you to talk to for advice, support and friendship. And we have made so many friends from these groups and many have become lifelong friends. It's been really lovely and positive for us as a family to have this kind of support behind us.

Having a great support network is so important and we are blessed with the people around us. Having support online has been amazing too with the many groups we are now part of. Seeing older children with Down syndrome and connecting with their families when we've wanted to ask a question has been wonderful. We have made some great connections all over the world and I love hearing everyone's stories and being able to ask questions to people whose children have had some of the same experiences.

We were also very fortunate to get therapy services quite quickly after Lucas was born. Because of the stroke he had, they were very quick to get us linked in as soon as possible. So, from eight weeks of age, Lucas has had physiotherapy and occupational therapy, and they work together. When we first began these therapies, it was once a month, but as he is growing and getting stronger, they are now every two months. He's progressed really well with the physical therapies.

Lucas has hypotonia as well as hypermobility, which is why he is struggling physically with things such as standing. It has taken him longer to do some things, and this is where the physical therapies can help.

Lucas has been provided with equipment to use at home, starting with a tumble form chair to aid him with sitting. He now sits independently, and we no longer have the chair but it enabled him to progress to a corner seat and it's these fantastic pieces of equipment that led him to be able to independently sit.

At the moment we are working on leg strength to help Lucas start to stand. We have a Therapy Bench which he loves to sit on and with this we encourage him to reach down for toys and pick them up. This has helped his balance tremendously.

And we also try to encourage him to push down with his feet to prepare for that big stand when he does it.

Lucas also has a standing frame, orthotic boots and made-to-measure gators which are like splints to help keep his legs straight and stop him bending at the knee whilst in his frame.

It has a tray where the top can come off and there's a bowl underneath for him to do messy play or water play so he can be distracted whilst standing. This also helps to build the strength up in his legs.

He goes to speech language therapy and has been attending this from a young age. We began this therapy early as he was having trouble with feeding (breastfeeding). We didn't realise that he was actually silently aspirating, so fluid was going onto his lungs, and this is also why he was having trouble with his breathing.

As he becomes older, we are working towards helping him more with this and hope that it will become easier for him in time. He can drink liquids, but they need to be thickened with a powder and because of sensory issues and oral aversions he doesn't really like the thickened liquid.

Lucas, Aged 2 Years

This has led to him refusing to drink and resulted in IV fluids from serious dehydration.

So, to help with his feeding and drinking he had a nasal gastric tube that allowed his feeds to go directly into his stomach. Because this is ongoing, and the tube quite often will come out and also cause discomfort from the tape on his face, he recently received a PEG.

Now his face is clear and the feeds go via the PEG directly into his stomach. The PEG is a new thing for us and we are getting used to it, but it's much better than having a tube and tape on his face. He also can't pull the PEG out as easily as the nasal tube.

It's not much fun having to go to hospital all the time, so the tubes have become a part of him for now. Having them saves the aspiration and frequent trips to the hospital.

It wasn't easy having this done and I actually had to get quite angry and tell the hospital and doctors that enough is enough. We can't keep doing this, it's not safe for him. I begged them to please, let us have the tube so he can feed easily without any danger so he can begin to thrive.

We have high hopes that as Lucas gets older, we will be able to teach him to drink orally and he will be able to have the PEG removed. For now, this is the best option for him and us as a family.

One of the reasons we are hopeful for this is because he does eat food orally. It is soft foods for now as he is only young but being able to give him the solid food allows him to keep the function of chewing and swallowing. So, we keep trying and we will see how he goes with it all.

It doesn't really matter though. As long as he is safe.

We still continue to encourage Lucas to eat orally so he doesn't lose all the important oral skills. At the moment, he will only eat pureed foods, but we are slowly introducing a lumpier texture which he seems to be accepting.

We also offer Lucas finger foods, and a lot of the time he will put the food in his mouth but seconds later spit it out. That's if he doesn't outright launch it across the room, no matter where we are or who we are with. It does make us laugh and this probably encourages him to keep doing it, but it is funny at the time!

Even though this happens every time we offer it, we still try every day because one day he will just get it. Sometimes these things take time and practise, but that's okay because the skills are there and with persistence every single day, he will one day just eat.

Even with the therapies and extra things we do with Lucas, he is such a cheeky little boy and beyond cute even if I say so myself. He also understands a lot more than people would think.

He is very loving, caring and gentle. He loves everyone around him and really enjoys playing with his older brother and sister. Lockdown affected things socially for him in the beginning because, like everyone else around the world, we had to stay home and couldn't visit anyone.

It affected Lucas because he became very clingy. We couldn't give him to anyone else when we first began to socialise again. If we did pass him to someone, he would just cry and try to get away from them. It was hard because it included family as well as close friends, but they understood.

Lucas, Aged 2 Years

Since things have started to change and restrictions have been lifted, he has come along in leaps and bounds socially. He loves to socialise with everyone and will now go to anyone that wants to give him attention.

Everybody that meets Lucas immediately falls in love with him. It's lovely to see others enjoying spending time with him, and he loves the attention.

Lucas is very sensory and likes anything with lights, vibrations and noises. He also loves material things and in particular, labels. If someone were to give him a label, he would be so happy and play with it for hours on end.

He's recently learned to roll a ball back and forth with his brother and sister and he loves this. It's quite fun to watch him reach a milestone like this. He loves to play with his brother and sister and follows them everywhere like a little puppy. He just wants to be around them and get involved in whatever it is they are doing.

His favourite things to watch are Cookie Monster from Sesame Street, Mr Tumble and Bluey. What kid doesn't love Bluey?

Cookie Monster was a favourite quite early on, and like most kids, he laughs at his antics. The whole show is great and just like his brother and sister, he loves watching and listening to all the songs. The bright colours really attract his attention too.

Lucas is such a great little boy who is full of life and fits into our family perfectly. It does get hard at times especially with getting referrals. We have a lot of following up to do with our paediatrician just to get the referrals and it gets frustrating because we need them so we can keep on top of everything for Lucas.

There are some hospitals that have multiple Down syndrome specialists whereas with the ones local to us, they only have one. Sometimes it can feel like you get a little bit lost, and a little bit forgotten about. There can also be times where you find you're just chasing up and trying to push the referrals and make sure they are there.

All in all, it's mostly been positive experiences we've had with all the medical professionals and whenever we have needed something urgent, it's been there. Sometimes it's a bit of a battle, but the advice and care we have received has always been wonderful.

As I said earlier, they put us in touch with some great supports that we continue with today and we have also met some wonderful families that have now become friends for life.

The support we have has been very inclusive because we all help each other, but I do worry about what will happen when he begins school and wants to participate in anything in the future. I really just want to make sure he is involved and included.

Next year, we will apply for him to go to nursery. The hope is that he will go to the same nursery his sister and brother attended. I want him to be included in what the other children are doing and for him not to be segregated.

In saying that, I totally understand that there are going to be different means and ways to teach him, but overall, I just want him to do what the other children are doing. I want him to be involved. Sometimes, modifying something slightly so he can be involved is all that may need to happen, and my hope is that things will be put in place so he can be involved.

Lucas, Aged 2 Years

I want the other children to want to be involved with him and socialise with him too and understand he is a person just like they are. I understand there are times when things are going to be different for him because they have to also be able to meet his needs. But I don't see why he can't be accepted for who he is even is he does need some extra assistance.

I just want him to be treated equally for who he is. I think that's our hope for all our kids with or without disability.

Please also know that you can talk to Lucas. Don't ask me questions or talk to me about him, talk to him. Interact with him. He doesn't talk yet, but he understands what is being said and by speaking to him, you recognise him as a person, and it will also help him with communication.

To me, if you don't talk to him, it feels as though you don't see him, and I don't want him to ever feel as though he is not there in other people's eyes. So, see him and talk to him. Get down on his level, talk to him and treat him like you would a typical child because he is a child with the same wants and needs as any other two-year-old boy. Don't ignore the fact that he's there and talk to me like he doesn't exist, because he does, and he loves it when people interact with him.

Everyone that meets Lucas instantly falls in love with him, but sometimes they still talk to me instead of him. I want people to communicate with him on his level because he will be older one day and he won't understand why people don't talk to him. Talking to him even at this age, will help with socialisation and communication skills for his future.

Also know that Lucas is very capable. Even though he is behind on his milestones, and he's not yet where a typical child might be, he is still capable of doing those things. It just takes him a little bit longer to learn and master the skill.

He's taking the scenic route, but it doesn't mean he's not going to achieve it. With love and support from us as well as the assistance he receives with his therapies, he will achieve. He is capable of learning, and he is capable of achieving. It doesn't really matter in our eyes how long it takes.

It's always important to give people a chance and the guidance they need. If you don't do that, then how are they going to learn?

Lucas is no different. He is our little boy, and we have the same dreams and aspirations for him as we do for his siblings.

We will give him every opportunity to do whatever it is he wants to even if it means thinking outside the box to find a strategy for him to participate or spending additional time with him to ensure he has a chance to learn and achieve.

You can follow our adventures here and enjoy watching Lucas grow as we do:

Facebook - https://www.facebook.com/OurlifelovinglucasT21journey - Award Winning Blog with a BAP award (Bloody Awesome Parent Award)
Instagram - https://www.instagram.com/our_life_loving_lucas/
TikTok - tiktok.com/@kerryannbellamy

Lucas, Aged 2 Years

IZZY AND SARAH
Southhampton, England

Izzy, Aged 4 Years

Isobel was born at 39 weeks and six days. One whole day ahead of her due date.

My husband Stuart and I, were not worried about anything leading up to the birth of our second daughter. During the 12-week routine scan, one of the things the sonographer checked for was the thickness of the nuchal fold. However, due to the way in which Izzy was laying, an accurate measurement couldn't be taken. We then opted for the blood test to provide more certainty around the 'risk' or 'chance' of the syndromes, Down, Edwards and Patau.

A week or so later Stuart and I headed to our local maternity unit for the blood test. On the way we talked about what we would think and feel if the test came back indicating Down syndrome. To be honest I don't think either of us knew much about the other two syndromes and so our focus was on DS.

What if the test told us our baby had Down syndrome? Our main thoughts were around what that diagnosis would look like for our family. Our older daughter, Tilly, was four years old at the time and we talked about the impact having a child with a disability would have on her. We also definitely talked about the option of termination.

The blood test results came back as 'low risk'. I believe we had a 1 in 250 chance of Izzy having one of the syndromes. If I think back to this now it is 'low' but four years earlier with Tilly's results, it was a 1 in over 1500 chance. I've often mused about those numbers. In hindsight, the difference seems important given what was to come.

The next milestone in many pregnancies is the scan at 20 weeks. For most, it's an opportunity to make a big decision – do we find out the sex of our baby? Stuart and I are curious humans, and maybe a little impatient, so we wanted to know. The sonographer confirmed there was no doubt we were having another girl. Stuart beamed at me. It was his lot in life to be surrounded by ladies.

However, the 20-week scan isn't just to confirm the sex of the child – it is also another opportunity to make sure the baby is developing correctly. It was during this scan that we were referred for a further appointment to review Izzy's heart. The sonographer at the 20-week scan could not quite make out all the chambers of her heart and so a week later we once again went to the maternity unit for a scan just of our baby girl's heart.

The scan was completed by two professionals. One experienced and one trainee. The results revealed all was well … again in hindsight, this seems amazing given what was to come.

The following 19 weeks passed by without event. I sorted through the items of clothing I had kept from when Tilly was a baby, deciding which were the most special to pass on to Izzy. We went right to the wire decorating the nursery, only finishing it when I hit the 38-week mark of the pregnancy.

I was 39 weeks and 4 days when I expressed concern to Stuart that our baby wasn't moving as she had been in recent weeks. We headed to the maternity assessment unit for monitoring. Everything was fine. After several hours we headed home with the advice from the midwife ringing in our ears – any more concerns about movement and we were to come straight back in.

And that is what we did the next evening. Izzy had stopped moving again and so we went back for further monitoring. Once strapped up to the monitoring equipment it was clear our girl was fine. She started to move about and her heart rate looked strong.

The doctor examined me and confirmed Izzy's head was engaged and she would give me a 'sweep' to get things going (no need to explain what a sweep is I hope). We were once again sent home and asked to come back the next day for a scan just to check everything was okay.

The next day the scan revealed that there was a lack of water around Izzy and the placenta was not quite working as it should. Clutching the scan results we went back to the assessment unit and without further delay we were ushered on to the ward for review.

Izzy began to quickly show signs of her heart rate decelerating and within hours we found ourselves rushing towards an emergency caesarean section.

Whilst this was not how I hoped Isobel would come into the world, the c-section followed the same experience as giving birth to Izzy's older sister, Matilda. Both babies had experienced a deceleration of their heart rate. The rush to theatre to meet Izzy safely was a little stressful but when she was born, she looked fine.

She was quickly taken for a newborn examination and within minutes there were two neonatal doctors talking to Stuart and I at the top of the operating bed. Theatre is a very noisy place, and I was very much under the influence of the caesarean drugs and so I didn't hear exactly what they said and I only caught the words 'syndrome' and 'features'.

We returned to the labour ward and the midwives were doing their usual checks, encouraging skin to skin contact and I was trying to breastfeed Isobel. Whilst the midwives were upbeat and Stuart and I were admiring our new arrival, there was definitely an underlying feeling of tension in the room. Something wasn't being said. And not just by the midwives but by Stuart and me.

We had both heard the neonatal doctors express something wasn't right. We waited for the midwives to leave, and Stuart and I immediately debriefed. We looked at Izzy. We looked at each other. I can't remember who said it first but one of us said, 'Do you think she has Down syndrome?' We knew. We just knew.

The two midwives returned to the room and continued to be bright and breezy about their work and then a consultant came into the room and very abruptly asked to examine Izzy. She wasn't friendly at all, she didn't smile, and I don't remember her saying anything like 'Congratulations'. I handed Izzy over to her and she started to bounce her up and down on her leg, she examined her feet and her hands, looked at her face.

I watched with a growing sense of fear. There was a knot growing in my stomach and my breath was quickening. What was this very serious woman going to say? There was an eery silence in the room as if everyone knew what was about to happen. The consultant asked me if I thought Isobel looked like myself or Stuart. Do you think she looks like your older daughter? I could feel the tears welling up in my eyes as I betrayed Isobel and said 'No'.

I felt like I had been exposed in that moment as a monster ... I felt that question was framed to shame me. 'Admit it!! You don't think she belongs in your family!! How could she when she looks so different from you all?' To this day I believe that consultant to have behaved in the cruellest way by asking me those questions. After I had answered her, she quickly said 'I have 30 years' experience as a paediatric consultant, and I am 99% sure that Isobel has Down syndrome.' Those words hit me like a truck and I fell apart within seconds.

The 99% became 100% two days later when the blood test confirmed the extra 21st chromosome. It was a different paediatrician who gave us the formal diagnosis of Down syndrome. He was a lot kinder than the first one.

We were taken into a room with a box of tissues on the table. The writing was on the wall. The doctor explained that Izzy would need lots of input from professionals and medical attention, but he also said, 'It's as much about the family that she's born into as anything else. It's the love she will get from you that will matter.'

I recall that I was in bright pink, plaid pyjamas, I was not wearing a bra. I felt very vulnerable. I was sobbing. I felt scared. I felt like this shouldn't be happening to us. It crossed my mind 'maybe we could give her up for adoption'. I felt like I wouldn't cope with a child with a disability.

I thought we would never go on holiday again as it would be too hard. I imagined the staring from others in the street. I contemplated behavioural issues and being judged as a bad parent. You name it I felt it. Some people look back on their reaction to the diagnosis and say they feel guilty about how they reacted, but I don't feel embarrassed or guilty about how I felt. I want to remember. To hold on to those early feelings because if another parent ever comes to me for advice, I want to provide comfort that they are feeling exactly what they should be, and it is fine. I don't want to deny my past feelings as they have shaped me today, and I am okay with who that is.

Izzy, Aged 4 Years

In those first early days we were moved to the neonatal ward for a nasogastric tube to be inserted. This was because Izzy was struggling to feed, and there followed a diagnosis of a complete atrioventricular septal defect (complete AVSD), which would require open heart surgery at some point and then hypothyroidism.

It was easy to feel entirely overwhelmed by what felt like an assault on my senses. The diagnosis, the further health concerns, not being able to breast or bottle feed Izzy, frantically expressing so she could have 'the best start', listening to new and foreign sounding language around the medical conditions, the support and help we would need … it was emotionally draining.

And then you have to tell people the news. You can't keep it to yourself. But by the same token you don't want to tell people, because telling family and friends makes it real and there was a part of me that didn't want it to be real. In the immediate hours after Izzy was born and the consultant had delivered her blunt and cutting prediction of Down syndrome, we had spoken to our parents and siblings.

My mum's reaction was fine, she didn't care that Izzy had Down syndrome. Stuart's Dad, brother and sister dropped everything and came straight to the hospital and wanted to help in any way they could. They immediately asked us 'What do you need?', 'What can we get you?' It felt like a warm blanket enveloping us, keeping us safe.

We texted some key people. These were the ones we wanted to let know that Down syndrome was a possibility. We did this to allow our immediate family to have others to confide in. Close aunties and cousins.

Once the diagnosis was confirmed we knew we wanted to tell a wider group of family and friends. There is a way you want to say it. You want to scream it; you want to sob it. But ultimately, I just texted them. I texted because it is easier. I knew that by writing it down I would be able to contain the emotion.

I look back at the messages I sent, and it makes me sad … I was trying so hard to be confident and strong, but I remember just feeling like this happy moment was ruined. I wrote the messages with tears streaming down my face. Alone at night in my hospital bed with my new baby downstairs in the Neonatal Department, and my eldest daughter and husband at home.

I do not think I have ever felt so lonely in my life. I remember thinking, this is going to be so shocking and sad for them all.

Without exception our family and friends sang in a chorus of love. I think the best way to explain this is to show you some of the messages we received from them.

'… even more reason to celebrate because she will show us all how strong she will be, she will be incredible, and she has just the perfect family to bring her up …'

'You have a daughter who will be brought into a loving supportive family … love to you all.'

'… we are looking forward to meeting our new Great Great Niece …'

'… can you tell Izzy that Great Uncle Nigel would like to have a cuddle and say hi …'

Izzy, Aged 4 Years

'Isobel will be so special to us all, looking forward to my first cuddle.'

'… seen latest pictures from Becca and love her already … really excited and looking forward to meeting her soon …'

'She is your daughter … she will thrive and be loved and that's all that matters.'

'You and Stu are amazing parents; your daughters have a very happy future ahead of them.'

'She's the best. Love her most!'

'I cannot wait to meet her and give all the snuggles …'

'What a beautiful baby girl you have been blessed with … I don't know enough about Down syndrome but Isobel will teach us all as we watch her grow.'

They weren't shocked and saddened; I was.

As time went on, I would repeat the words 'Izzy has Down syndrome' to as many people as I could. I found myself bumping into people we knew or being stopped by a lovely old lady whilst she rhapsodised over how cute Izzy was. I would quickly say, 'Yes she has Down syndrome'. I would say this before even mentioning her name.

I was like Mufasa from the Lion King, holding my baby aloft and declaring to the world 'SHE HAS DOWN SYNDROME!' Sometimes people would look at me surprised or confused as to why I was telling them. But for me there was a force stronger than myself that meant I needed to repeat the words, I needed to desensitise them.

We left the hospital with Isobel after 10 days. We left armed with a copy of the pack from the Downs Syndrome Association, we had training on how to manage the NG tube and how to resuscitate her if we needed to, she did after all have a serious heart condition. I mean, that's not the typical experience of having a newborn is it? That's as far from 'normal' as you want to be as a new parent. I recall being given a t-shirt with the key points of resuscitation on it. We put it on a cuddly teddy bear and kept it in the lounge in case we ever needed to refer to it. We still have it.

In the first few months post-birth I was looking for support and comfort and the first resource was the Downs Syndrome Association pack. It was a very worn set of documents by the time I was ready to stop looking at it. I would pour over every word, seeking reassurance, looking for the words that would tell me life would not be so different from how it had been before Izzy was born. I did find comfort; and I didn't.

There was also an online support group called 'Designer Genes'. This group was made up of parents with a child Izzy's age and it was good to read their posts. It did help but I remained in the background, rarely breaking cover with my own questions or concerns. If I wasn't ready to engage with an online support group I certainly didn't feel strong enough for any face-to-face groups. And more than that I didn't want to go.

If I am honest, I didn't get involved in the support groups on and offline because if I did, I would be admitting to being part of this world now, part of this community. And I didn't want to be. I didn't want any part of it. I couldn't imagine what I would have in common with any of these strangers.

By the time I think I may have been ready for any face-to-face support groups, we were plunged into a world of persistent hospital admissions, as Izzy began experiencing numerous chest infections. So, I guess it just never materialised that way for us as a family. We all find support in different places, and it is important to find your own way.

Friends suggested some online blogs to follow. There were two that stood out to me. I found Sarah Roberts and Oscar with the Don't Be Sorry page early on. I read her posts avidly. I felt her journey of diagnosis and the way in which she explored her emotional state at that time, was similar to mine. And I looked at Oscar (who would have been about five at the time) with his sparkling blue eyes, and swathe of blond hair and thought to myself, 'Yes. I can do this. It won't be so bad.'

The other blog I discovered was 'Frankie Says Relax About T21'. Written by Donna Jackson with her daughter, Frankie, front and centre. I enjoyed the 'zero fucks' attitude Donna had, and I felt emboldened to face whatever came our way. These two blogs talked about the positives but also touched on the challenges in a way that was understandable and digestible for me. These two blogs provided me with a lifeboat in the storm of my mind. I would read their posts and know that I was going to be okay. That Izzy was going to be okay.

One of my most enduring friendships came about unexpectedly, when Izzy was about five months old. It was a couple of days before World Down Syndrome Day on 21st March 2018 and I was doing my usual morning sift through my favourite bloggers' pages when I noticed 'Don't Be Sorry' had posted a video of a bunch of children with Down syndrome, sat in their cars with their parents, they were signing along to the Christina Perri song, 'A Thousand Years'.

I watched it over and over, the tears coming thick and fast down my face. This video had some sort of guttural kick to it. Here were these children, possibly four or five years old, they were exchanging so much love with their parents. I looked at the parents repeatedly ... they were happy. They were proud of their children. They loved their children. I was moved beyond words. Once again, I could feel hope surging in me for a future that would be okay.

One of the parents in that video was Stacey Byrne. I had heard this name before. A friend of a friend had mentioned her months earlier. Stacey lived local to me and had a child with Down syndrome. The suggestion was for me to contact Stacey and we could talk about how I was feeling. Well, needless to say I never got in touch with her. This would have been even worse than a support group in my mind. I did not need any new friends and I certainly did not need any friends within the Down syndrome community ... what would we possibly have in common?

However, Stacey had other ideas and shortly after the video went viral she set up a charity called 'Wouldn't Change A Thing' (WCAT). The charity also offered an online support group. In June of 2018 Stacey reached out to me. I was ready. It was time. I was mentally and emotionally starting to come out of the fog. We chatted on Facebook messenger a little and I joined the support group ... and I surprised myself by actually getting involved! Izzy and I also became part of the awareness raising that the charity went on to do over the coming years.

Izzy, Aged 4 Years

We signed in videos, and we supported their campaigns whole heartedly on social media.

I am no longer connected to Wouldn't Change A Thing. For me it wasn't anything dramatic. The relationship just soured, the messaging, the vision just became an untenable fit for us as a family.

However, I am grateful for the time I spent in the WCAT family. At the time, during that period of my life, it was exactly what I needed and the message of 'Wouldn't Change A Thing' was very important to me. I have no regrets about anything we did, and it did serve a purpose for us as a family. But in the end our lives went off in a very complicated direction and I could no longer hand on heart say I wouldn't change a thing, because there is a lot I would. And WCAT could never find a way to properly represent our family dynamic. They tried but their very mission statement butted heads with our reality. They are not alone.

Many of the other high profile support groups and charities are hellbent on presenting only one, sanitised version of life including a child with Down syndrome. Their motivations for this vary, but what does not vary is that our family unit does not fit their narrative.

But the best thing WCAT brought to my life was Stacey. And because of that friendship I have other friends who are amazing and so supportive. I have finally found the support group I needed.

A couple of weeks after Izzy's first birthday she was admitted to hospital for the first time with a respiratory infection. It came out of the blue. We ended up staying in hospital for 22 days. Izzy returned home but she needed to be on oxygen all the time. We would ping in and out of the same hospital many more times in the months that followed. Izzy just couldn't cope with any chest infection. We exceeded 50 days in hospital between the end of October 2018 and the beginning of March 2019. Some admissions were just an overnight, others lasted weeks

No-one tells you when you have a child with Down syndrome that they might get very ill. That they will be hooked up to oxygen to help them breathe. That you will become familiar with the names and faces of all the doctors and nurses on a particular ward because you have bounced back in and out so many times. That part is left out.

It was exhausting.

I missed life as it had been. I feared the pull of the hospital walls, drawing us back in and making me face how much life had changed and how ill our daughter was. And I felt I wasn't doing any part of my life justice. Having to explain to my employer that I would have to miss work again because we were back in hospital with a poorly child. Missing our older daughter, Tilly, terribly. It was tough.

But in March 2019 we felt hope that we would turn a corner with Izzy's health. We checked in to our local hospital on 6th March for Izzy to have her heart condition, the complete AVSD, repaired. It was scary but exciting. This surgery would fix our baby girl's little heart, and this would mean we could avoid those gruelling stays in hospital. Life could finally return to normal. How naïve of me to have made that assumption. The surgery went ahead the next day, 7th March. It went well, really well and Izzy was out of the Paediatric Intensive Care Unit (PICU) within two days.

Izzy, Aged 4 Years

However, two days after that Izzy went into respiratory and circulatory collapse. She had septic shock. We returned to PICU with an incredibly poorly little girl. Her temperature was 42.8 degrees. She had to be wrapped in a freezing cold cooling jacket and put on a ventilator to breath. It's strange how the same four walls, the same machines, can feel so incredibly different to how they had four days earlier.

With the heart surgery we had been prepared. We had seen pictures of other children (posted in the support group pages) who had had the same surgery as Izzy. In the hours after open heart surgery, there was an element of control. We had known what to expect – it was planned. This time there was a sense of panic; Izzy was very poorly. All I could see were the tubes and wires and our tiny daughter fighting the fight of her short life.

After a few days Izzy began to improve; the cooling jacket was removed and she was taken off the ventilator. However, something was very wrong. You see when Izzy had come round after her heart surgery, she was sitting up within 12 hours. She could focus on us and whilst quiet, she seemed to be herself. This time she was not. It was quite evident within minutes of seeing her that things had changed. She was lying down and was quite floppy, there was certainly no strength to sit up as she could barely move her arms and legs. Her eyes were crossed, and she was focused on the ceiling.

The doctors explained that this could be a normal reaction to coming out of sedation and said that they would keep the neurology concerns in the background if things didn't improve.

Neurology? The seed was planted. This seed grew into an almighty tree of concern by the end of the day. With each passing hour that Izzy didn't come round properly, the branches of that tree spread and a blinding panic tightened its grip on me. Every time a medical professional came to examine her I would cry. I was imagining the worst, the worst being that Izzy had suffered some sort of brain damage.

The panic reached epic proportions as Izzy had three or four 'episodes' in as many hours. During these episodes she would become very stiff, arch her back and her beautiful little face would crumple into a twisted knot of pain. This was accompanied by a cry so horrendous I thought my heart would break for her.

A neurologist came to see Izzy. He appeared out of nowhere and clapped in Izzy's face. I was tottering on the edge and this exercise (to see her reaction to stimulus) reduced me to a mess of snot and tears. An EEG was performed which showed no sign of seizures, and another neurologist reviewed Izzy's notes.

The conclusion was that this response was typical of a child who had had lots of sedation and morphine and was effectively in withdrawal. Our minds were at ease ... well sort of. After all, who wants there 17-month-old baby to be going through withdrawal? But at least withdrawal would pass ... right?

The next day I headed off to collect Tilly from her dance classes and returned to the hospital to allow her to visit her sister for the first time since we had been admitted. On my return it was once again clear that things were not right. Izzy was still quite unresponsive and the 'episodes' had continued throughout the day and were increasing in frequency.

Izzy would ball her fists, straighten her arms, roll her eyes in to her head and then her rate of breathing would increase

Izzy, Aged 4 Years

(thankfully she had stopped crying out in pain). This was now happening every couple of minutes and in order to investigate a CT scan was ordered. However, because the team needed Izzy still for this to happen, she had to be reintubated and put back on the ventilator.

We waited anxiously for the results and then the doctor came to see us. The CT scan showed evidence that Isobel's brain had been starved of oxygen, there was a brain injury, brain damage. They didn't know when this happened, and they didn't know the extent of the damage. The neurologist would review Izzy's CT scan in detail and talk to us as soon as he could.

Stuart and I cried. The nurses pulled the long blue curtains around Izzy's bay. When you are in PICU and you see that happening it either means personal treatment for the patient or privacy for a family who have experienced bad news. You never want to be the latter, but here we were.

Stuart informs me that my legs gave way beneath me. I was crouched on the floor, gripping the bars of the cot, and emitting a sound I don't think I have ever made … crying, groaning. Stuart and a nice nurse got me to a seat and the nurse talked to me. 'You don't know what this is yet. You don't know how this will look. Children's brains are very good at rewiring themselves.'

We needed space and we headed to the PICU waiting room. I grabbed Tilly and took her for a walk in the corridor whilst Stuart updated his sister. Then Stuart sat with Tilly whilst my sister-in-law and I went for a walk. What do you do when you have been told your child has a brain injury? That there is brain damage? You walk, even though it is raining, you cry, even though you thought you had no more tears, you smoke, even though you shouldn't, and you throw up (in a bush opposite the car park entrance).

What goes through your head when you are told that your child has brain damage? You see the last picture you can remember taking of her as clear as day … she is beaming into the camera wearing the blue and yellow crown knitted for her by a friend's mum. And you already miss that smile because you think you won't ever see it again. And you curse yourself. Because you wasted far too long worrying about Down syndrome and not enjoying her. Because you allowed yourself to indulge in 'woe is me' instead of appreciating every day you had … because you believe, in that moment, that you won't get back the little girl you have come to adore and love.

The next day the neurologist came to see us. He showed us Izzy's CT scan. We could see the darkened patch on the right-hand side of her brain, at the back. We were taken to the quiet family room. Isobel had had a stroke in the part of her brain that controls sight. Izzy would probably have some visual impairment but should make a full recovery. He remained convinced that the 'episodes' we were witnessing were as a result of withdrawal and it would take time for this to stop.

He was wrong. The episodes did not stop. They got worse. We came to understand that Izzy had developed a neurological condition called dystonia, and later we would find out she had suffered a global hypoxic injury. The impact of these two conditions had wreaked havoc on Isobel physically and cognitively.

Dystonia is a debilitating condition that takes so much from those who have it. It steals comfort. It invokes pain – in the early days of Izzy having full dystonic episodes she would scream in pain. Because of the global hypoxic injury Izzy could no longer sit up, she had zero head control, she could not clap, wave or high five like she used to. She did not smile for what felt like an eternity after the stroke.

Izzy would require a lot of therapy and support following her brain injury. I remember in the early days of life with Izzy, thinking that all the therapists and specialists Izzy was seeing was excessive. I mean at six weeks old she had representatives from nine different disciplines looking at her. Why did she need a dietician? Of course, I was wrong. Izzy very much needed all those people paying attention to her but sometimes it felt intrusive.

We had a special health visitor, speech and language therapist (SALT) and physiotherapists, who would come to the house. They would complete a little session with her and then I would have to continue with the therapy when they were gone. I felt I couldn't make decisions for her as her mum. The dietician told us how much to feed her and when. I wanted to shout, 'I just want to breastfeed my baby! Why can't I do it! I physically ache from not being able to do it!'

Izzy would regularly pull out her NG tube and we would have to have the community nurses come to the house to replace it. We couldn't just care for our child alone, we had to have lots of people involved, asking questions, making suggestions. I know it sounds incredibly selfish and I realise lots of people struggle to get the support they need for their child, but I just felt all this attention was a reminder of how 'different' we were now as a family.

Izzy's physiotherapist recommended a specific chair for her to sit in, a Tumbleform. On the day it arrived I burst into tears. It was huge. It would take up too much space and it looked very medical to me (although it was plastic and could be easily cleaned which was a massive bonus given how bad Izzy's reflux was).

I can laugh at this now. Post brain injury our house is bursting with equipment to support Izzy around the house day to day. And I love it all because it helps our girl to engage in our family life, it presents opportunities for her to build on her rehabilitation. I also love talking to her therapist at her school and learning about what we can do for Izzy.

Izzy goes to a school for children with profound and multiple learning disabilities and I love interacting with the team there, because they are so clever at engaging her as an individual. I listen and learn, taking bits of what they do into our home to work with Izzy on. As Izzy gets older, and with what we have gone through, I can see how these therapies fit together now.

In the beginning I always felt very bewildered and like I was playing catch up trying to understand things, constantly on information overload. These days I feel part of the team, like I am actively involved in Izzy's development and not just a bystander.

Izzy is an incredibly sweet little girl. She adores cuddles and getting attention from her big sister. When Tilly is in the room, Izzy only has eyes for her. Izzy loves dogs. We've got a dog and my mum has five dogs (I believe my Mum is the mad dog woman). Izzy will literally open her mouth to let the dogs lick inside her mouth. On every single level, it's disgusting, but it's also quite sweet because she cannot coordinate her hands to stroke them so that is how she's trying to get attention and show

Izzy, Aged 4 Years

affection with the animals. We also have two cats at home, one of the cats is totally in love with Izzy and when she is napping on the sofa, Jacob (the cat) will lay on her and sleep.

Izzy also loves to be part of whatever we are doing. When we go over to my mum's, we will play board games. Whilst Izzy cannot actively get involved, we can sit her by us and she enjoys watching our reactions to the games. We can give her choices, so we might position her between us playing and the television. She might choose to ignore us and watch one of her favourite animated movies – she loves Croods 2.

Izzy also loves watching game shows, I think it's the lights and noises that make her so happy. And not to forget how much she enjoys sensory toys. Things like light toys, bubbles, jingle bells and her space blanket.

It's so important to pay attention to what Izzy is communicating without the use of speech. Her body moves in certain ways if she is happy or sad, her noises change with her mood. We want Izzy to be included in as much of our family activities as she can be, that's not always physically possible but recognising that she is enjoying an experience doesn't mean watching her pick up a bowling ball, it is recognising the joy she gets when we go up to her and celebrate that we have knocked the pins down (often just one in my case).

Our friends invite Izzy to their birthday parties, and they will tailor the party bag just for her, she gets bubbles and sensory toys.

Inclusion for me is knowing that someone must have a seat at the table whilst understanding that not everyone might pick up the pen to write. Regardless, the opportunity must exist.

Our journey so far has been split in to pre brain injury and post – the 84 days we spent in hospital following surgery a sharp intersection in our lives. When we returned home as a family of four for the first time after our harrowing experiences in hospital, we were relieved, but the unknown of the future would press down on me for many years to come.

Even today over three years later there are so many unknowns. Izzy has still got such a long way to go in her recovery, and the truth is she may never get back the abilities she had before. But what she can and can't do becomes less important with the passing of time and the realisation that regardless of that, she is very much her individual self and is loved for that.

Page Mentions:
https://www.facebook.com/dontbesorry2
https://www.facebook.com/frankiesaysrelaxaboutt21

Follow Izzy and Sarah here:
https://www.facebook.com/FeelingUpsideDown

Izzy, Aged 4 Years

LINCOLN AND STEPHANIE
Mount Keira, New South Wales, Australia

Lincoln, Aged 6 Years

'You have a decision to make …' were the first words we heard before even receiving our diagnosis of Trisomy 21 at 12 weeks. There was no explanation at that point as to what we were needing to make a decision about, just that we needed to make one.

We had been booked in to get the results of our 12-week scan and were doing a follow-up appointment with our obstetrician who also happened to be our fertility doctor.

Our first child, was basically a honeymoon baby, however, falling pregnant the second time around wasn't so 'simple'. After just over a year of trying we engaged some assistance from the local fertility clinic. We were very fortunate with the first round working and we were so excited to be having another child.

I remember walking into that appointment. It's still very vivid in my mind every time I recall that day, and the emotions, at times, are still very raw. The office space was lovely, it overlooked the mountains and on that day the light was shining into the room and it was warm and bright. The doctor was sitting at his large desk looking over notes on his computer. My husband and I took a seat on the opposite side of the table and waited. All of a sudden, the pen he had in his hand dropped to the table with a thud, accompanied by 'oh' and he turned to us and said, 'You have a decision to make.' These were the first words he spoke to us on that day, I don't even remember a hello when we first walked in.

We asked what he was talking about, to which he replied, 'You don't know?' We asked again what he was talking about, he didn't realise we were unaware of any results. The words that came out of his mouth next were, 'The baby has a high chance of having Trisomy 21.'

We had no idea what that was and when we asked, he told us it was Down syndrome. I sat there for a moment trying to recall what I knew about Down syndrome, my brain trying to make the connections to what it was, who I knew? I was in my own little world in that moment.

He interrupted my train of thought and said, 'Oh, you look like you're about to lose it.' I remember that really irked me at the time and told him I was just trying to process what he was telling us. Looking back on it, that was probably the first time advocacy kicked in. Who was he to question my thought process about my child? It was a strange and uncomfortable few minutes with so many emotions running through my mind and body. Ben and I were constantly trying to read each other's thoughts.

Then came the words, 'I'll book you in for an amniocentesis.'

'No, that's not happening,' escaped my mouth before my brain had time to catch up to what was coming out. I was adamant that I wasn't going to have an amniocentesis, after trying for another baby and knowing there was a high chance of miscarriage with having an amnio. I didn't want to risk it, no matter how he tried to reframe it. Instead, I told him I would do the harmony test even though I knew it wasn't diagnostic testing, as I also wanted to know whether we were having a boy or a girl. A formal diagnosis wasn't going to change our decision to progress with the pregnancy. Our baby was our baby, a diagnosis wasn't going to change that fact. I was already thinking whatever is going to happen will happen, or whatever is going to be, will be. When and if challenges presented themselves throughout our journey, we could address them then.

I asked the doctor if he was able to connect us with any other families locally who had a child with Down syndrome. There was actually another family locally who had also just received a diagnosis, however, due to confidentially we weren't able to talk to one another. He didn't have any connections nor resources for us to take away. Genetic counselling wasn't offered but he did recommend the psychologist he was seeing if I wanted to 'talk' to someone. That was the only support that was offered and he gave me the woman's phone number. I texted her and explained why I was making contact, but I didn't hear back from her.

'Now, treat this like a business lunch, don't talk to each other about what you're thinking or feeling. Order a nice meal, enjoy it and then, after that, each of you let the other know what they are thinking.' As we sat, heads racing, in shock, processing, wondering, scared, hopeful and so many more emotions and thoughts, the doctor told Ben that ultimately the decision was up to me, and he should support me with whatever that decision was. I thought that was a strange thing to say, but figured he was going down the line of my body, my choice.

When we walked out of the doctor's office, the receptionist wanted to book me in for our next appointment. I had essentially been composed when we were in with the doctor, but everything came to a head once outside. I was trying so hard to hold back the tears, but they just started flowing. I told her we had just received some news and I was trying to process it, I would need to call her to book in our next appointment. I just wanted to get out of that office as quickly as I could.

We had a divided response from family and friends. For the most part they were amazing, and I will be forever grateful for their love and support. However, some found the diagnosis very difficult to come to terms with mostly due to their outdated views of T21 and fought, pleaded and begged us to change our minds (the same people now, who love him with all their heart). Then, there were others who thought that it was their duty to tell us how THEY felt and that if we didn't agree with them then, we obviously weren't thinking straight, hadn't thought things through or weren't making an informed decision.

We were told:
'What about your other son, you really need to reconsider for his sake.'
'This news is worse than my own baby dying in my arms.'
'You're a fucking idiot for not terminating.'
'I'm so sorry.'
'I'll pray that he doesn't have "it".'
'I don't think you fully understand what you're getting yourself into, this will ruin your life and your family.'
'I don't know if I could do it but I think you're amazing.'
'I don't think you have looked at all the outcomes.'
'You are going to have to look after this baby 24/7 for the rest of your life and who is going to look after him when you're long gone?'
'Wow! Really? Wow! We were in a similar position last year but everything was "okay" our baby was "normal" otherwise, we would have terminated.'
'Are you sure?'
'Well you should have considered that this was a possibility due to your age?'
'Why are you the 1 in 10 that isn't terminating?'
'OMG, that's so terrible.'
'So is it because of religious reasons you're keeping "it"?'
'When did you find out?'
'Did you have an amnio?'

'You're only looking at the positives! Of course these families are saying positive things, it's their new "norm", just like it will be your new norm.'
'I'm surprised you're going through with this as I thought you were a perfectionist and I didn't think you would be able to handle a child with a disability.'
'They are only cute when they are little.'
'You're such a strong/special/amazing person.'
'You'll love your baby.'
'They are so happy!'
'It will be really tough, stay strong.'
'You're so blessed. God doesn't give you more than you can handle.'

I felt as though I had to justify my son's life, defend him and fight for him not to be judged. The thing is, for anyone one of you out there reading this who has a child …
Do you not love them unconditionally?
Do you not want the best for them?
Would you not do anything to protect them?
Do you not suffer when they suffer?
Do you not rejoice in their laughter and beaming smile?
Does your heart not burst with pride for your child?
Do you not rush to their defence when there is an injustice?
Do you not want to keep them safe?
Do you not love your children equally?
So why should I be any different?

The day that people stop saying sorry to families when they receive a prenatal or postnatal diagnosis is the day, we are being inclusive.

A couple of weeks passed, and I received a call from the doctor with the results of the harmony test. Before he could even begin,

Lincoln, Aged 6 Years

I told him that if we were going to proceed with him being my obstetrician for this pregnancy, his bedside manner needed to change. I told him the way he handled things on the day we were there, was not acceptable. He apologised and told me I was right and that it was something he was working on.

He didn't remain my obstetrician because at the 20-week scan Lincoln ended up having quite a large AVSD, so we were then referred to the Royal in Sydney and they took care of us until Lincoln was born. They were lovely and very supportive through the whole process and the geneticist was surprised at how well we were coping with everything, considering we had a lack of support.

I googled and searched for Facebook groups at that time, desperate to connect with other families. I called Down Syndrome NSW, but they weren't able to connect me prenatally. Unfortunately, I didn't come across the 'T21 Mums Australia' page then either which would have been such a comfort for me, especially in the middle of the night when I couldn't sleep and felt as though I couldn't breathe. I would cry for what felt like hours, my heart felt like it was being ripped out of my chest and my stomach in my throat. I would cry not because my baby had Down syndrome but because of how he was already judged by those closest to us.

At 20 weeks pregnant, the diagnosis of a very large atrioventricular septal defect (AVSD) and tetralogy of fallot (TOF) like restriction on the pulmonary artery led us on another journey with the most amazing cardiologist called Doctor Steven Cooper. He is the most beautiful man and an exceptional communicator. I remember leaving the first appointment with him in tears because it was the first time we came across someone so supportive and nurturing.

Our experience with Dr Cooper was the polar opposite to what we had experienced with the Trisomy 21 diagnosis. He personally came and greeted us in the waiting room. He was a softly spoken man with such kindness in his eyes and so much compassion. After a while of chatting at his desk, he stood up and came to our side of the table, asked if we minded if he sat in between Ben and I and told us everything that was happening with our unborn baby's heart, even drawing a picture to help us understand it all. This was a scary time for us, not knowing if he would survive the pregnancy, birth or be given the lifesaving surgery he would inevitably require when needed.

I agonised over not knowing if my baby would survive the pregnancy, if he would be stillborn (because that's what I was told by the doctors on several occasions during a check-up appointment), if his heart would be able to cope once he arrived, if he survived. Furthermore, how society would treat him? Would he have friends or a girlfriend? Would he be okay long after we were gone? Would our eldest cope? How could I protect him, keep him safe from all the trolls out there?

So much angst. Then, so much joy!

I was booked into the Royal Women's Hospital in Randwick to be induced with Lincoln around 37 weeks. I had gestational diabetes and was on two metformin tables plus insulin three times and day and over 150ml at bedtime. It didn't seem to matter how strict I was, it just didn't want to budge.

Arrangements were made to be induced so that the team were on hand to manage any complications that may arise. It was February 21st, the day before Nate, our eldest, had turned 10. We left for Sydney late afternoon and at around 6pm I was induced.

Lincoln, Aged 6 Years

The nurse told us if things weren't progressing by around 7am, they would most likely break my waters. My husband was able to stay in the room with me, on a rubber mattress on the floor and it was around 10pm when my contractions started. By 12pm they moved me down to the birthing unit.

This birthing experience was very different to my first, I guess because:
a) I knew what to expect, as far as giving birth goes.
b) I was very conscience of trying to remain as calm as possible.

I wanted to birth naturally, which I had done with Nate but this time I was more prepared, more in control, more focused on my breathing. I had to be. I had to do all I could to make his entrance into the world as stress free as possible. My internal mantra throughout the labour was, 'Calm mummy, calm baby.' I needed to do all I could not to stress out the baby and his little heart.

Due to it being the middle of the night, the staffing that they had told me needed to be on hand, weren't. I did have my beautiful midwife, Maria who had been with us throughout the pregnancy and she really was the only one (apart from Ben) present, until his little head popped out. I remember being asked not to push at this stage as they had called for the doctor to come. Now, for anyone who has felt that urge to push, let me tell you it took everything in me to remain focused on baby and not pushing. Things were very quiet in the room, and I thought something was wrong, his head was out but no noise, so I asked, 'Is everything okay?'. Maria reassured me and told me I just had to hold on and wait for the doctor to arrive before pushing again. I believed her and soon enough the doctor arrived. Shortly before 3am, Lincoln made his glorious debut, earthside.

They quickly whisked him to the corner of the room to check his vitals. Lincoln was breathing well, he wasn't blue, he was here and okay! While they were weighing him, I caught a glimpse of him from a distance. I remember thinking how perfect he was and, in that moment, all the doubt and fear that had lingered was washed away.

They put him on my chest, and he made his way to my breast immediately and began to feed. It was the most wonderful moment. They gave us a few minutes with him alone. Once they left my husband let go, he had been so worried for him throughout the pregnancy and through his tears told me how relieved he was that he was here and safe.

After we had some time together, they took Lincoln to the NICU, and Ben went along with him. We knew that this would be the case and we had been given a tour before he arrived to help us prepare.

Everyone at the Royal Women's Sydney hospital were wonderful and so supportive. I had some cookies made up for the nurses because I knew we were going to be in hospital for a while. Every time a new nurse would arrive on shift, I would give them a cookie to have on their break, our way of saying 'thank you' for looking after Lincoln.

They were all surprised how well we were handling everything, especially him having Down syndrome. I told them we knew about his diagnosis since I was 12 weeks pregnant. We had spent the pregnancy on an emotional rollercoaster and now, it was time to simply enjoy our baby. He was perfect, just like our first son, Nate.

Lincoln, Aged 6 Years

It was easier for me to breastfeed Lincoln because I had breastfed my first, so knew what to expect and didn't have the stress of needing to learn that or being told which way to hold him, place his mouth, wet the top of his head if he falls asleep, et cetera. It wasn't as stressful or such a concern like it was the first time around. It was something I really wanted to do with Lincoln and was so pleased that, despite being told otherwise, when pregnant, I was able to breastfeed him. I was also a lot more assertive with the nurses when it came to feeding and what my expectations were. There was only one nurse who kept on sneaking formula to Lincoln when I wasn't around and I had already caught her twice doing this and after being ignored, let the head nurse know who rectified the situation and it didn't happen again. I had been expressing even before he was born due to my gestational diabetes and had a good supply of milk. A friend had given me her sister's breast pump and it was such a time saver! There was loads of milk ready for Lincoln in the NICU fridge and I continued to pump so he could be fed breast milk via a nasogastric (NG) tube. Due to his heart condition, he would get tired easily, so we had short breastfeeds and would top him up via the NG.

During the first couple of days, it was hard to walk and in order to be with Lincoln it would require someone to come and take me to the NICU via a wheelchair. It wasn't on the same floor, and we had to go down a level. This was hard, not having him with me or being able to see him when I wanted. Having to wait to be taken to him. Mostly, this happened in the middle of the night as during the day my husband and I spent most of our waking hours with him. Ben had booked accommodation nearby and my parents watched our eldest for us, bringing him up on weekends to spend time as a family together.

I had been discharged after around nine days of being in hospital. I then joined Ben in the accommodation he had been staying in nearby. On this particular night Ben went home to Wollongong (about an hour and twenty minutes away) to see Nate. In the early hours of the morning, I awoke with a high temp and was in a lot of pain. I managed to drag myself into the shower and by some miracle walked to the hospital, all the while crying. Late during the pregnancy, I had cellulitis and it had returned. When I arrived at the NICU, through the intercom I stated I was unwell and didn't want to see Lincoln just in case I had something other than cellulitis but was pretty sure that's what it was. They were wonderful and immediately had me examined, and within a short time, popped a canular in and I was on antibiotics. They readmitted me into the maternity ward, so I was able to still be as close as possible to my baby.

Lincoln spent 13 days in NICU until his oxygen levels dropped and they let us know he would require surgery and they would have to do an incision on his side to place a 4mm Blalock-Taussig (BT) shunt, which would assist with blood flow to pass through the lungs, so he would receive more oxygen. This would allow some more time until he was ready for his full repair once he had reached a certain weight or once again his saturation levels indicated it was time.

Surgery wait time was hard, but I was surprisingly calm. Maybe too calm. Completely focused on keeping it together. If I didn't and started to crack, I would fall into a heap. Ben and I watched a movie in my hospital room until the call came to say, surgery had been a success and we were able to go and see our baby.

He was now in the Intensive Care Unit (ICU) across in the Sydney Children's Hospital. It was connected to the Royal, there are a few that are in a block. We made our way over but had to wait a couple of hours before they would let us in to see him. My family, parents and grandmother had all driven up from Wollongong to see him. Together we waited, then finally Ben and I were allowed to see him and Nate came too. Including Nate in that initial visit was probably not the wisest idea. It was very confronting seeing Lincoln post-surgery. He was sedated, completely naked, breathing tube in, wires everywhere, catheter. Two nurses always by his side. A lot to take in for an adult, let alone a child but we had no idea what we were walking into and perhaps if a nurse had suggested we didn't bring Nate in until we had seen Lincoln, maybe we would have taken on their advice.

We spent the next 10 days by his side in the ICU. We weren't able to pick him up and it was 'nil by mouth', which meant I continued to express by his side. When we left the ICU, I had a massive esky full of breastmilk. At the time, I had wanted to donate some of it but wasn't able to due to protocols. The staff were incredible in the ICU. There were always two nurses with him, and they constantly kept us updated on what they were doing and how he was progressing. With every little thing they did, they would let us know. We were allowed to stay as long as we wanted with the exception of an hour in the morning when they encouraged us to go and eat breakfast.

On a Monday, in the parent's room of the NICU at the Royal the social worker held a little support group for parents whose baby was staying in the NICU. It was an opportunity to chat with other parents about what had happened during the week with their babies and depending on what procedure they may have had, (X-ray, blood test, canular, extubation, hi-flow, etc.) we were given a corresponding bead to represent our child's journey. The program was called 'Stella Beads' and coincidently, the woman who founded it had a little girl with Down syndrome. I didn't learn this until a couple of years later. It was a time where we had the opportunity to connect with other families on the ward and not feel so isolated. It was also such an eye-opener to a variety of diagnosis and procedures.

After ICU we were sent to the children's ward where we spent the final time waiting for Lincoln to recover and feed before we were able to be discharged. We were in hospital for a total of four weeks. The doctors needed to be sure he was able to feed from the bottle (even though I was breastfeeding) for complimentary feeds, as he needed to put on a certain amount of weight, and he would still get tired from a breastfeed because of his heart condition. It took around three months of a combination of bottle and breastfeeding before he was able to be breastfed successfully. Breast shields made a huge difference and once weaned off those, he was breastfed until he was around 18 months when he started biting me and I weaned him off.

Once discharged we spent the next few months going to weekly appointments with Lincoln to check on his incision and have the dressing changed until it was healed. Also, to monitor his saturation levels. This was done so we knew when he would need to have the full repair on his heart.

In between the time he needed to have his repair, we also started in-home therapies with Lynne, his beautiful physio and lovely Amy, his speech pathologist. They would visit together and through play he was getting stronger and hitting milestones along the way. We started doing Key Word Sign with Lincoln around six months, and Ben and I attended a one-day workshop where we started using some of the signs applicable to what he was needing/doing at the time and included that into our routines.

Lincoln, Aged 6 Years

Amy also taught us games using KWS, so we were able to do this repetitively with him during activities.

Around eight months he was booked in for his full repair and we headed to Westmead Hospital for the incredible Dr Orr to perform the very complicated (due to the size of his hole) surgery. We had booked an apartment close to the hospital for a month as they said it would take a few weeks for him to recover.

The night before his surgery we stayed in the apartment as a family and had to bath him in a special solution in preparation. Early the next morning, we headed to the hospital to hand him over to the doctors. Only one of us was able to take him in. I held him and sang twinkle, twinkle little star as they placed the gas mask over him, and his little body went limp in my arms. I kissed him on his beautiful little head, told them to take care of my beautiful boy and they escorted me back to Ben and Nate.

We were told the surgery would take around six hours and not to expect to hear from them during that time, but hours passed by and nothing from the hospital. Around seven hours in I called to get an update. They weren't sure where he was ... they would need to call me back ... seriously? Finally, someone got back to us and said he was still in surgery and would be a few more hours. They would call us when we were able to make our way over. Surgery ended up taking 10 hours as his tiny heart was a little twisted in its position, which needed more time. His recovery was amazing, our little warrior was in and out of hospital exactly a week from when he went in, and we were going home!

Friends and family would often comment during the pregnancy about how having a child with a disability would affect his brother, Nate. Would they have asked the same question if

Lincoln had been a post-natal diagnosis? I do have regrets around how we delivered the diagnosis to his brother, who was only nine years old at the time. There had been many tears and visitors to our home soon after we were given the diagnosis of T21 and at the time, I thought that Nate may be wondering what was going on and why we were upset.

We ended up playing him the clip 'Dear Mum' on YouTube. He was having chicken broth at the coffee table and we cast it to the TV, telling him we wanted to share something with him. We told him his little brother was going to be like the people in the clip. He watched it in silence, I don't remember noticing any facial expressions changing during it but when it was over, he was dead silent, processing it, just like we had back in the doctor's room. He didn't finish eating and after a while asked why we showed him the video? I told him that he may have noticed that we had been upset the past few weeks and that there were people coming over more often than usual. Perhaps he had wondered why? He replied he hadn't noticed. Why did we feel the need to share this with him … was it really necessary for the little boy to take on the same stresses we had been feeling?

A few days later when Ben walked down to the school to pick him up and while they were walking home, he asked Ben why did our baby have to have Down syndrome? Ben replied that it was just 'mother nature' and the way it is sometimes. He said he wanted to do this to mother nature and held up his middle finger. Not something we were expecting and certainly not the type of thing we went around doing but straight out of the mouth of babes … it was raw, it was honest, he just wanted the best for him.

It was hard enough for us to process at the time and here we were putting the same worry onto him at such a young age. He didn't need to know. His brother was going to be his brother, no matter what and he would love him unconditionally. He wouldn't have known any different if we hadn't shown him that video.

The year Lincoln was born, there was a disability competition across primary schools and Nate came home with the following poem he had written at school and entered into the competition. He ended up being a finalist.

FIREWORK

Lincoln is a Firework he shines bright
Even with Down syndrome he puts up a fight
His arms, legs and cheeks are so puffy
And he always loves to do fluffies.

He loves to scream and shout with joy
A shaky rattle is his favourite toy
When he farts and he is stinky
Me, mum and dad call him 'stinky Lincy'.

We take Lincoln to hospital appointments every week
There's a hole in his heart and it makes him weak
He's having his second operation at the end of the year
If it all goes well, we get to keep him here.

He has 47 chromosomes instead of 46
But it's not a problem that I want to fix.
I really, really love my homie
Even with an extra chromie.

– Nate Rodden, Age 10 Years

Love doesn't count chromosomes.

From the Hearts of Mums

When Lincoln was about a week old, a young mum walked into my parents' variety store in Nowra, with her daughter Hayley who, was just under one year and happened to have Down syndrome. Mum struck up a conversation with Kyia (mum) and told her I had recently had a little boy with Down syndrome. They exchanged details and Kyia made contact via Facebook and connected me with the T21 Mum Network Australia.

This was my first experience with the online support world and forums. I was linked in with other mums within the Down syndrome community that had babies born the same year as Lincoln as well as a group with a variety of ages. It was amazing!

Within the first year of Lincoln being born, I approached Joelle Wedd who had founded T21 Mums Australia and told her about our diagnosis delivery, lack of support and pressure to terminate the pregnancy. I told her I was an educator and a photographer and asked what she thought about a book being created that could be given to doctors to show families at the point of diagnosis. It would be a book with families from all over Australia for people to look at and read the heartfelt quotes with the images. I thought that would make a big difference to families receiving a pre or postnatal diagnosis and felt it was something that I could help bring to life.

For me, that was what was missing at the point of receiving the diagnosis. Having connections to other families. I wanted to see images and hear stories from other families with children of all ages. I wanted to be able to share beautiful imagery of people with Down syndrome being celebrated with their families. I wanted families that had just received a pre or postnatal diagnosis to have the opportunity to connect with families around Australia. For these families to be gifted a copy of this book by their medical professional at the point of diagnosis so they were able to have something beautiful to look at and read.

She was very open to the idea and let me announce the book project within the private T21 Mums Network group. From that, the first book was born, and I founded the social enterprise, 'Celebrate T21'. T21 comes from Trisomy 21 which is the medical term for Down syndrome, hence, celebrating T21 and its community.

Since launching in 2017, we've created three beautiful photo books which celebrate the lives and experiences of families who have a member with Down syndrome, through sharing wonderful photos and heartfelt stories. Our first book was published in 2018, and we published a UK version for British charity Wouldn't Change a Thing in 2019, followed by a third book in Australia in 2021, *Celebrating Down syndrome. Changing the world one chromosome at a time*. Our fourth book, *Your life. Your way. We're here*. will be released in 2023 and we will also be travelling the country with a stunning art gallery that will showcase families in our most recent book and also feature the designs by the super talented Alexis Schnitger who creates all of our shirt graphics and elements. She is also known for the T21 arrow that went viral, with people around the world getting a tattoo of the arrow.

We've distributed more than 4,000 gorgeous photo books to date and also gifted over 350 gift packs.

Throughout this journey, we have met the most incredible people within our T21 community and made some of the most wonderful friendships. That is something I hadn't expected or thought about when pregnant. It truly is a beautiful, supportive community.

It's true, what they say, 'Once your baby arrives, you'll wonder why you worried about the diagnosis so much.' For us, that was definitely the case.

Lincoln 'fills our cup'. The way he can light up a room, change a mood and the amount of love that he emulates is such a unique and magic experience. Sometimes it's a look or a movement that's made and your heart is filled to the brim with love. I love how these emotions extend to people outside our family, too.

In life we have no control as to what cards we are dealt but we do have control as to how we play our hand.

Do we know what the future holds for Lincoln? No! Just as we don't know what it holds for Nate. The only thing we do know with certainty is that we have two boys whom we love and cherish dearly.

We feel so much more joy, love and happiness now that our little family of four is complete and as far as decisions go … we all have a decision to make. How we communicate, react, respond and treat one another. My decision was to rewrite the narrative around Down syndrome and Celebrate T21.

Follow Celebrate T21 here:
Facebook - https://www.facebook.com/celebratet21
Website - https://www.celebratet21.com/

Lincoln, Aged 6 Years

Images – Bobby Kidd Photography

CASSIE AND ELLEN
Beechworth, Victoria

Cassie, Aged 7 Years

At first sight we were so in love with Cass.

She was gorgeous, she was ours. She had my bright blue eyes, my mum's ears, and my husband Lindsay's smile. The memory of how enamoured we were in that moment shines brightly through a cloud of an enduring birth, painkillers and the uncertainty building within as I suspected that our little girl might have Down syndrome.

My mum had worked in both aged care and disability, and through her work I became familiar with many of her clients, who would always stop to chat with us when we saw them down the street. This plus an outdated pamphlet we received from the doctors when we did our screening test were the sum of our knowledge on Down syndrome. Looking sweetly into our daughters' eyes I noticed an upward slant and while touching her soft hands noticed the gap between her thumb and pointing finger.

My husband and I discussed as we cuddled her and decided to wait until the doctors had come to look at her rather than worrying. We decided to focus on the fact that she was such a beautiful little baby girl and enjoy that moment.

We could hear the midwives chatting amongst themselves but not saying anything much to us at all. Then around 9am that morning, the paediatrician came in. He was lovely, chatting directly to us and asking how we were going.

He then calmly told us the midwives had advised him there were possible indicators Cassie might have Down syndrome, which after cuddling, cooing and checking her over he agreed. He said he was pretty certain, but he would organise a genetic test to 100% confirm the diagnosis. He asked for our permission to complete the test, and then reiterated his congratulations, that she was gorgeous and said he would send someone to talk to us later that day.

I sat there completely overwhelmed, I was still in recovery from her birth after being in labour for around 50 hours, forceps delivery, and still hadn't slept so my mild amount of worrying before we saw the paediatrician spilled over. I was awash in anger and tiredness from the birth, euphoria from our beautiful baby, grief from the journey expected and drowning in questions, questions I couldn't answer, ones I shouldn't have to answer right then and there but as someone who has anxiety and likes to plan my mind, I had been sent into full swing. Questions like, 'Am I enough?', 'Does she have any heart problems?', 'Will she have to go to surgery?', 'Does she have bowel problems?' We are in regional Victoria, so I was starting to worry about having to go to Melbourne into the Children's Hospital if anything was wrong. By breakfast I was already on to questions planning 10 years ahead.

Everyone who knows me knows I am a crier; it is a way I process emotion. I cried at my wedding, most parties, and that day I cried just the same as I processed everything going on. My main midwife was amazing, positive, and very kind. But as the other midwives came around for check-ups and seeing my teary, snotty face would continually say 'sorry' and seemed undeterred from my replies that I wasn't sorry.

It was not because Cass had Down syndrome that I cried.

Lindsay was an unwavering rock, all he could see was our amazing daughter, and his trademark 'it'll be fine' attitude was both a source of annoyance and support as we readied to let our family know. We had made the call to ring them and tell them before they arrived so we could chat to them individually on the phone rather than a big muddle all at once which as we predicted came to fruition with everyone arriving at the exact same time.

I'm so grateful for my family because it was them that brought me back down to earth. They were helping me to settle down and enjoy her. Stop planning which primary school she is going to go to when she has only just been born. Don't worry about things like that, there is time.

I cannot deny that initially I was worried about how things would go when they came in to see us because of the shock, but they were all amazing. I needn't have worried at all. None of them expressed sorrow and they all embraced her for who she was right from the start. There were tears, but I'm sure it's because they could see how emotional I was.

They asked questions about what we had already been told and kept telling me what we were thinking all along. That she was such a beautiful baby.

My mum was one of my biggest supports right up until the day she passed away. She was the one that told me about how to look for Better Start and Early Intervention. The doctors didn't tell me, the midwives didn't tell me either.

It was so strange because the paediatrician seemed to expect the hospital to tell me what was next. And the hospital expected the genetic counsellor to tell me what was next. Everyone assumed we had been told and nobody checked or questioned it.

Cassie, Aged 7 Years

We returned home a few days later, no surgeries, just another ultrasound in a few days' time to make sure the newborn holes in her heart had now closed. I think maybe because we didn't have those added things happening, everyone thought we were fine and knew what the next steps were.

We didn't have many connections where we live so I was extremely grateful for the support from my mum and family. My sister moved up from Melbourne not long after Cass was born to be closer to Mum and us. She has been wonderful with Cass, and we've grown a lot closer after we lost Mum and she was blessed with her own kids.

My friend Amy is amazing. She thinks of my kids as her own and even has them as desktop wallpaper on her computer. Amy and my other friends have always been wonderful with Cassie. They've been curious which is fine, and they've always asked questions.

The questions have not been what you would think, they have been more about asking what we need. What supports do we need? What milestones is she up to? And they celebrate the achievements of Cass just as much as we do. It's wonderful to have such a great network of friends.

I did try some mum groups, but it never felt right. They behaved very strangely around us and asked some questions which were probably said in innocence but were very off putting. My maternal health nurse kept pushing for me to join a supported playgroup but instead of explaining it was a way for me to engage with other parents of kids with disabilities, it was sold as somewhere that Cass belonged like she didn't fit anywhere else. It made me very stubborn towards it, which is something I really regret.

It wasn't until Cassie was two and we were walking through a craft market that a lady tapped me on the shoulder and asked if she could give her a gift. I thought it was strange but didn't think it would hurt. She gave us the gift and told us she had a daughter with Down syndrome and then she disappeared.

We walked around the market hoping to find her and we did. Here she was at a little biscuit stall, and we started talking. The person with her was the head of the local Down syndrome group which surprised me as I had never even heard of it.

We did attend their group, but due to work, inactivity and after moving to Beechworth after my mum died, it was hard for us to get there at times. I didn't connect back then as much as I'd have liked to, but I am now in contact and working with Vanessa (head of the group) to get things active again.

I found support online by accident, I think I saw a post somewhere and followed it back to the T21 Mums group. The online groups have been great, even though sometimes they can feel a little overwhelming depending on the dynamics of the group. Some personalities can be very dominant and at times it can be difficult to voice questions and concerns.

When we had the opportunity for Cassie to be an ambassador with Celebrate T21, I realised that I could add a lot of value as a contributor to the group.

I felt very welcomed right from the start, and I think that gave me the confidence to do more and be part of everything. It's been great because the support is online, so it is accessible for us in regional areas where there is not as much face-to-face support.

Cassie, Aged 7 Years

Down Syndrome Victoria didn't contact us for almost two years. When they finally got through, they still thought she was a newborn and were quite surprised when I told them she was almost two.

Cassie was a great baby. She was very settled, eyes open and smiling from day one. I know now the early smiles may have been wind, but we loved them, nonetheless. It was very hard not to fall in love with our gorgeous girl.

We have gone through different doctors over time with her and they've all been pretty good. There's only been a few where we felt as though we had to ask them questions to clarify certain things.

We've had to advocate a few times because they've immediately blamed Down syndrome for certain things when we know it's not that. Quite bizarre sometimes really and I always felt strange telling doctors they weren't right, and they needed to look closer.

We've been lucky in our home town because one of the doctors we see has a brother with Down syndrome and she understands and looks closer when we have queries. It can be very frustrating seeing different doctors all the time because we always must go right back to the start whereas with this doctor, it's been much easier.

With my other kids, the doctors get straight to the point with everything but with Cassie we always must go over everything right from the start. Sometimes she just has a cold like her siblings, but they always want to dive in deeper, even if there isn't anything to dive in deeper for.

I understand history is important, but going backwards with them to move forward gets so repetitive, even with doctors who do seem to understand. So when we found our doctor, it was wonderful. She's hard to get in to see, but we will wait when we can because it's always so much easier.

It's another reason why I'm so glad I found Celebrate T21 as it's such a supportive group and I wanted to be able to be part of that support for other families.

In being proactive with finding supports, we've done well, and have some great people in Cassie's life supporting her. I'm thankful to my mum too because without her, we may still be trying to navigate things. She had the knowledge and passed it onto us.

We found a speech therapist for Cass that we accessed at the time through Scope, and she is still her therapist now. She is amazing and works well with Cassie and us as a family. She also helped us as her key worker as well as organising further supports and being a strong advocate.

We started physio early with Cassie as well but after some time that dropped off because she did so well with her physical development, and now she has regular occupational therapy sessions. That, with the speech has been great for Cassie and we have also now found out she has level 3 autism. This means it may take even more time for her to reach goals such as speech, but because we have that diagnosis, we receive greater support.

We have bought lots of resources for her and they work great for her speech and her being able to let us know what she wants and needs.

Cassie, Aged 7 Years

The school she attends is very supportive of her needs and the therapies she attends. They have a few teacher's aides who all engage with Cass and have developed amazing bonds with her. I love how excited they get showing me photos of all the things she has done that day.

They are also very proactive in learning how to use the resources we have for Cassie. I really loved this, because it showed me that they really did have an interest in what was best for her. I didn't have to make a time and try and to teach them how to use them. They had already taken the steps.

Early schooling was interesting for Cassie. We had her enrolled at Montessori for the kinder program they had. It was a lovely school but so under resourced in areas of disability. It is because it's a private school and the funding they do receive cannot be used for an individual student. It must be used for the whole school.

Because of this we were unable to get an assistant/aide for Cassie and she needed that one-to-one element at least to keep her on track and assist with her communication with her peers. It was a huge barrier and became very evident quickly.

She ended up being very isolated in that kinder environment as she was kept separate from all the other children. They told me it was because they couldn't keep an eye on her properly while playing on equipment and other things like that.

Because of this, the other children didn't play with her. She only seemed to be allowed in one spot and they didn't want to go there all the time. The school also were not helping with engaging conversations between Cassie and the other children.

I also felt as though the school weren't communicating with me properly. They would just keep telling me she had a great day and never brought up any problems that were obviously happening. I could have assisted them with resources to make things easier for Cassie, but they never expressed a need for anything like that.

I remember one of the teachers telling me once about Cassie washing windows all week. She said, the only thing Cassie wanted to do was wash windows. I asked why nobody would tell me something like that. Why would they just let her do that rather than encouraging her to stay on track with the program?

I also later found out of another time when she wanted to build a tower with blocks. What happened was that they ended up pulling her away from the activity because she wasn't doing it the way they wanted her to do it. Cassie stopped going to the blocks after that because she felt as though she wasn't allowed.

We found that because of the way they had pulled her away from that activity, if they ever wanted her to do something there, she wouldn't go because they had told her no. She found it very confusing that one day they are taking her away from the activity, and the next day they are wanting her to play there.

I still don't understand why none of this was ever told to me. I could have sent in one of her therapists to assist and help organise things for her to do. Those were the issues we faced while Cassie was there. It was a lovely school, and the teachers were lovely, but it wasn't the right environment for Cassie.

Because of Covid, the online learning and the things that happened at Montessori, we decided a public school would be the best fit for Cassie. At a public school we would be able to have an aide for her that the other school couldn't provide. We also asked the teachers at Montessori many questions before making the final decision like, 'What will you do for her?' and 'What will you change to make it better for her?' They said she would benefit if she did another year of kinder but because they couldn't answer my questions on why it would be better for her to do this, we left and chose the public schooling system.

Cassie wanted to go to school, learn and engage with the other kids and we needed somewhere that would assist us with the right pathway for this to happen. Once she started at the new school, the transition was amazing.

Within two months she had changed completely. She was engaged, socialising, she had a friendship group, she was speaking more at home with her voice, signing and using her PODD book. We knew we had made the right decision because of how happy she was and how engaged the teachers were. They were communicating with us all the time and updating us with her progress and any queries.

Cassie does the same work as the other children, but she might have a slightly modified version. The end objective is the same, but she learns it by going on a different pathway.

I was so grateful we had finally found some more great support and resources for Cassie, and it was great to see her thrive.

Cassie is seven years old now, turning eight in October. She's a rebellious, tenacious and very independent little girl who knows exactly what she wants and how she wants it. Everything from the order in which I make her sandwich to how we turn the television on. She knows exactly how things are meant to happen. If we don't do things the way she thinks they should be done, she definitely lets us know very quickly.

She has a very vibrant personality that shines through with everything she does, and she is very empathetic. She connects well with others and understands everything that is going on around her. Sometimes she has a little trouble expressing her feelings because of the different way she communicates which is mainly through signing or her PODD book.

She does use verbal communication and one of her first words was 'no'. She was extremely good at telling us that.

She does enjoy a lot of television and can get a little obsessed with it. One of her favourites is Bluey and Bingo. She loves everything Disney and gets up and dances along with all the characters in her favourite movies and sings at the top of her voice and demands the music is put on in the car.

She is very good at creating her own signs for movies. Sometimes it takes us a while to know what she means, but we always end up working it out.

She loves going to school and when she wants to go, she points to the logo on her school top, or she will point to where it sits on her body when she doesn't have her school top on. And when she wants to go, she wants to go now.

She lights up a room when she walks in. Everything comes with such energy from her and even when she's sleeping, there is still something to see with the poses she gets herself into.

Cassie, Aged 7 Years

It's hard for me to describe her fully so people understand exactly what she is like for she is amazing.

She loves mirrors and loves to practise dancing and makes funny faces while watching herself. I think she wants to understand what she is doing with her body and all the funny things she can do. She loves to dress up and pretend to go out and about. She pops a hat on, checks herself out in the mirror and off she goes.

Facial expressions are a favourite to watch in the mirror and the poses when she dresses up. She is extremely theatrical in what she does.

I love the individuality she has and that she is her own person just like everyone else. We are all different and we all have different opinions on things, different likes and wants all depending on the life we live and challenges we face.

My wish for Cassie is to be part of her peer group and feel as though she belongs. That she and her peers have access to all the tools they need for effective communication and connection. I want her to be accepted for exactly who she is.

I've done two talks at her school to raise awareness about Down syndrome and answer their questions. I do an activity with the kids at the school when I am speaking with them, and I tell them I'm going to do a sign and they need to guess what it is.

I then tell them the first made up sign she taught us which was for 'Hotel Sylvania' and how it took us two-and-a-half months to work it out. She was trying so hard to communicate with us and we weren't ready. We were the ones that were behind, and we really had to step outside of our game and step up because she was ready.

She was trying to give us instructions and we just weren't ready. She is always two steps in front of us and we are always chasing her. She is teaching us all the time and I am then taking those learnings and trying to educate others.

There was also an instance where a child said, 'I don't want to talk to Cassie because she can't talk to me.' Through my talks and in working with aides we have worked with all her peers on the notion that a conversation is between two or more people, not one. That we needed to be ready to listen to Cass, that she has a lot to say we just need to know how to receive it.

We also worked on building additional resources for the kids to use, and continuing their understanding not only with key sign, but Cassie's own signs. Inclusion has many paths, and often people act like it only means that someone can move with everyone else unaided. I don't think that's entirely correct. I think it's more about ensuring that every person, no matter their ability has the resources available to obtain their goals, and no-one is left behind or left out.

She is completely integrated in this school and it's so wonderful to watch and see her as part of the community. Kids coming up asking her how her weekend was and asking about what she did. Trying to engage with her and encouraging her to share with them. It doesn't feel like she is to the side or separated. She is part of the community and that is exactly what we want for her, to be included.

I want people to know if you want to have a conversation with someone, you must also be part of that conversation. It takes an ear and a mouth to have that conversation. So, for Cassie, you have to be the receptor. You also need the knowledge to be the receptor.

To have an inclusive environment, we need people to be open to inclusion. To provide the resources and to allow our students to feel like they can have that communication. The schools are wanting to introduce Auslan into their learning and I think that would be a great idea. It would help for more people to be included in conversations.

We teach our kids how to integrate and how to be part of a community, but I don't think there is enough learning as a community to assist with this. We need to change the narrative so that everyone is trying to integrate, and people should also be teaching their children how to communicate with others and how to have relationships with kids with disabilities. That's an area that's not being targeted and I think it really needs to be.

Images - Love, Gem Photography

EVAN AND STACEY
Southhampton, Hampshire, England

Evan, Aged 8 Years

At the time we found out our son had Down syndrome we realised we knew next to nothing about it.

Our journey with Evan began as soon as I saw those two lines on the pregnancy stick. One of my close friends Nikki is a midwife, and looked after me throughout my pregnancy as she had with Evan's two older siblings. I remember her coming to my home and booking me in, talking me through the combined screening and asked if we were opting in or out?

As I did with my previous pregnancy, I opted in and ticked the box. No real thought went into it. You're wondering why? Because 'that' wouldn't happen to me so it wasn't something I needed to think about, right? Wrong.

Before we knew it the 12-week scan was here. We were so excited and couldn't wait to get there and see our baby for the first time. This was my husband's first baby (I already had two boys), so he was extra excited to meet and hear our baby's heartbeat for the very first time. However, it didn't go to plan.

Matt and I sat together in the waiting room excited, talking all things baby. We watched other parents coming and going with their baby scan pictures clutched in their hand, smiles beaming across their faces. We were smiling at each other thinking, 'us next'.

Before we knew it, off we went, into the room for our scan. We couldn't wait! I hopped on to the bed. Cold gel applied. I lay waiting to hear the magic heartbeat. And guess what? We did! We heard it. We heard it loud and clear. The most perfect sound, the beat we had waited weeks for. Followed by the silence.

Very quickly it became clear something was very wrong. The sonographer finally spoke, 'I need a second opinion. I need to call for a consultant.'

The joy of hearing the heartbeat vanished. We knew something wasn't right. She cleaned off the gel and ushered us into a side room to wait. You know, the kind of room that has a box of tissues on the table. The kind of room where you know you are going to hear something life changing. Yeah, that room.

We waited and we waited. It felt like a lifetime. No spoken words. We were in total shock. What could be so wrong? We felt sick to the stomach. Tears rolled. Panic had well and truly set in. What have they found? What's happening? What's wrong? What's taking so long? The warmth and exhilaration had drained from us.

After around 45 minutes the door swung open. A consultant appeared asking if he could re-scan me. 'Follow me,' he said. I found myself back in that same position, albeit laying on a different bed, in a different room (a 'better scanner' apparently) knowing there was a heartbeat but not knowing a lot else. I lay there nervous, fearful, vulnerable, in tears. Facing the fear of the unknown, waiting for someone to say something. Matt sat next to me with a look on his face like he was watching a horror movie unfold.

'Okay. I have double checked measurements; we should finish up here and go and discuss,' said the consultant. We were walked back to 'the room'. The box of tissues room, you know, the one where he will break the bad news, tell us what's wrong, give us the information that I knew we didn't want to hear.

'The nuchal fold on your baby's neck is significantly high. It's 12.3mm, which indicates a chromosomal "abnormality",' he said. He went on to tell us that our baby probably wouldn't survive. He proceeded to say that he had not seen a measurement like that for a long time. 'It's a significant measurement,' he said, adding the heart would most likely stop before 20 weeks' gestation. They had also detected cystic hygroma, indicating hydrops. Hydrops is a life-threatening condition in which a foetus has an abnormal build-up of fluids.

He advised us that termination is an option. I knew very quickly that termination wasn't an option for me and politely said no. Matt, my husband, looked so terrified he couldn't even talk.

All sorts of thoughts started filling my head with worry and fear. What on earth does this even mean? One of my first thoughts was, 'How will my other two children react to this? How do I start to explain it to them? How will this impact their lives? How on earth will they even begin to understand?' And then there is me, an older mum. 'Will I be able to look after a disabled child, when he's 20?' I will be on the road to 60. 'How will I do it?' And selfishly, I also thought about how our family would look to other people.

My husband, Matt, said to me afterwards that, based on the medical facts we were given, if it was his choice, he would have thought about a termination. Of course, he thinks totally different now, but at the time he was petrified, not about what the consultant said (he was giving us facts) but discovering so much was going wrong for our baby.

Once the consultant knew that we were not considering termination, we talked more. He talked through and explained we could have something called 'Non-Invasive Prenatal Testing' (NIPT). He explained that it tested for certain syndromes, Down syndrome (T21), Turner's syndrome (monosomy X), Edwards syndrome (T18) and Pateu's syndrome (T13). I knew nothing about any of them.

At this point he couldn't confirm which chromosomal condition my baby did have, even though he was pretty sure we were looking at Down syndrome. So, we opted to have the NIPT. It felt this was the natural next step for us without risking a miscarriage by opting for amniocentesis. We needed to know.

We made an appointment for two days later at a nearby private hospital. The test wasn't available on National Health Service back in 2013 so we needed to pay. We left that day very different to how we walked in, that's for sure. Unfortunately, we weren't offered any information or support so, as you can imagine, we headed straight home to 'Google'.

We started weighing up which Syndrome would suit our family best, searching pictures to see what our baby could look like. You know, for example, does Down syndrome look 'better' than, say, Turner's syndrome? Sad but true (not that it would have made any difference).

Two days later, we're back, drawing blood to be sent off to America, then the two-week wait.

Those two weeks were the worst two weeks of our lives. Unfortunately, that Christmas wasn't the one we hoped for. We'd had the test on December 16th. We were totally out on a limb trying to make sense of it all. We still hadn't been given any information, not even a leaflet. Just sent home to wait. We felt lost and alone. It was a heart-wrenching and confusing experience. We felt devastated, but we carried on googling. We felt we needed to. It gave our minds something to do.

Finally, while I was driving, the awaited phone call came. I pulled over. 'Hi Stacey, I have your results. I have bad news. Unfortunately, you are carrying a baby boy with Down syndrome,' said the consultant. I immediately thought 'bad news' who says that's bad news? Not me! I felt so much better knowing.

We opted out of any further testing as we knew our decision was made and this information was enough for us. I decided to tell certain people, starting with my children, then extended family and friends. I had lots of heads tilts, and heard lots of 'sorry' and 'are you keeping it?' which I expected. I felt the same when I was told. I was sad, worried and scared too, so why would I expect others to be any different?

Once our family and friends realised that we had chosen to keep our baby, attitudes started to change, and conversations started to become a little more positive but still worrisome due to Evan being so poorly.

My pregnancy continued, with many ups and downs. It was an emotional and fearful time, we discovered Evan had heart issues at around 20 weeks and continued under foetal medicine where they kept a very close eye on us both. We had many scans and were monitored very closely for the duration of my pregnancy. I'm not going to lie, it was a bumpy, emotional road!

We had around five months to find out as much as possible. We knew nothing. We'd never crossed paths with anyone who had Down syndrome. We only knew what our consultant told us and that was more the medical side rather than lived experience. I sourced Down syndrome support groups, talked to parents who had babies, children and adults with Down syndrome and started my journey with them. We're still on that journey with some of them today.

Evan arrived at 37.5 weeks, 6 June 2014. A normal delivery, four hours from start to finish. He weighed a healthy 7 pounds, needing no intervention, with only myself, Matt, Matt's mum and my midwife in the room. Breastfeeding was established right away. I cannot explain the joy in the room that day. There was an explosion of love.

Having the non-invasive prenatal test gave us time to process the news. It gave my other children time to ask questions, for the family it gave them reassurance that we wanted our baby and we were able to talk about the news in a more positive manner. We all started to learn about Down syndrome. For Evan, it gave him a chance to survive in the womb. Extra monitoring, extra scans, extra care through my pregnancy. Making sure everything was in place and that everyone that could be needed were on stand-by outside the labour room door. I felt my baby and I were cared for by all the professionals that day.

After many blood tests, tests and heart scans on Evan by doctors we took Evan home, just two days later, and introduced this amazing little bundle to his new family. His siblings couldn't wait to meet him. They were right away intrigued by Evan's features, especially his almond shaped eyes. They asked lots of questions, and after all the questions they settled right into being the protective big brothers they still are today.

The extended family felt love as soon as they set eyes on him. There were no 'head tilts' or 'sorry' just acceptance. Evan and his brothers welcomed another little brother into our family in January 2016, Olly. Owen, Sam and Evan are wonderful big brothers to Olly and Olly a perfect little brother to them. All four boys have such a special bond, the love and protection between them is priceless.

As time passed, Evan grew and progressed, walking, babbling and his cheekiness was shining through. Physiotherapy, occupational therapy and speech therapy became a weekly routine in our house. Evan wasn't keen. He loved his weekly play sessions though at our local SEN playgroup which incorporated therapy play to help and support his independence, and for me it was nice to meet other families who were living similar, complicated lives as we were.

Evan needed his first operation in December 2018, he had his adenoids and tonsils removed to see if that would help his sleep apnoea. Unfortunately, his symptoms didn't change and still he suffers from sleep apnoea today. Investigations are ongoing.

In January 2019, he had heart surgery and recovery was long. Evan style, there were a few complications along the way. In April 2019, Evan was admitted to hospital when a viral infection took hold. The viral infection turned nasty very quickly and he ended up in intensive care, intubated and very poorly. We did not know if we were ever going to be able to take him home. Whilst he recovered from this terrible illness, unfortunately, he suffered a significant stroke which has left him with life-changing side effects.

We eventually went home from hospital six weeks later. Once home we started intensive therapy, as the stroke took away everything – his personality, and everything he had worked so hard to achieve before the stroke. We witnessed him meeting his milestones twice over. He had to learn to roll again, sit up again, jump again, walk again, ride a bike and most of all get back to his cheeky self again. He has lost the use of his left arm; however, he is adapting well. The stiffness in his leg caused by the stroke saw him on the operating table once again, last year, in October 2022. Recovery is ongoing.

Evan did attend a mainstream school placement; we found his needs were not being met so we decided that a special educational needs school would suit him and his needs better. He absolutely loves school now and is thriving in his placement.

Evan enjoys socialising with his friends and is very cheeky with his teachers. He uses Makaton to communicate with others, however, by only having one arm/hand to use (due to the stroke) the Makaton signs would now prove difficult for Evan to use and to communicate for others to understand him universally. Many Makaton signs require two hands. That didn't stop Evan, he has adapted many signs, Evan style! We hope his educational journey stays positive as his journey progresses through the years, and he reaches his full potential.

At eight years old, he is well on his way, setting up a little disability awareness business, Brothers Creative Works, with his younger brother, Olly, who has autism. For many individuals with disabilities, pursuing traditional employment can be a daunting prospect, full of challenges and uncertainties. This frightens us as parents, and this is the reason why we want them to have purpose at a young age.

Overcoming challenges and developing confidence is vital, and this opportunity serves both for the boys. It also raises awareness of disabilities/hidden disabilities, gives the boys the chance to build something from the ground up whilst young and provides them with therapy, interaction, confidence and much more.

Teaching about disability helps to break social barriers and allows a better, holistic approach to inclusion of people with disabilities. Promoting awareness starts from home, a place where the positive attitudes, values and customs are reinforced on a regular basis. Home is dear to us, a place of comfort and understanding towards every aspect of life. As parents, we will do our utmost to allow our boys to experience a life they deserve.

As Evan grows up through the years, we hope his life becomes a little more settled, medically, physically, emotionally and within the wider world, as we do all our children. We hope he is included fully within society, for people to see Evan, Down syndrome, and all his qualities, strengths and weaknesses. The whole package.

Inclusion is important to our family. Evan was born with Down syndrome, and it's a big part of who he is. We should never overlook his condition; we are proud of him. We hope society embraces the word Down syndrome, and every person who carries that extra chromosome! He is different, but we are all different, we are all individuals with our own needs and wants in life.

On his next birthday, Evan will be nine years old. It has been a very long and tough 10 years, (including my pregnancy) for him and us. He has certainly packed a lot in and kept us on our toes, that's for sure. Throughout it all he has got up every time, shown true strength and determination with everything that has come his way. I pray he keeps getting up and myself, his

Evan, Aged 8 Years

dad and brothers will be right by his side, cheering him on. As we will always do for each other.

The love I have for Evan is strong, the mother instinct is strong, the protection for him is strong. I will advocate and fight for him for as long as he needs me to. I will shout from the roof tops every time he needs me to. My fuel will never run out all the time I am breathing.

Having Evan in our lives has been the most amazing, rewarding but worrisome journey, however, we have learned very quickly that all four children are different from each other and bring something different into our family life. Evan has done exactly that.

For me, it's been a journey where I came to learn about Evan and his condition, a journey of pure love, where we as a family accept each other, and value each other equally, despite our differences.

I had a choice when I was pregnant, and I chose to keep my baby. Would I go back and do anything different? NOT A CHANCE!

Our family is complete.

Follow Making Chromosomes Count – The DS Family News here – https://www.facebook.com/makingchromosomescount
Follow Evan and Olly's Business here - https://www.facebook.com/brotherscreativeworks
Follow their personal blog here - https://www.facebook.com/neverunderestimatemeT21

From the Hearts of Mums

DARCY AND JULIE
Langwarrin, Melbourne, Australia

Darcy, Aged 17 Years

Our journey with Darcy began long before he was born and when I look back now, it actually began before I even became pregnant with him.

In 2004 I met Tina Naughton when our eldest children were in class together at school. She has a daughter, Amy, who lives with Down syndrome, and I really enjoyed watching her play in the school ground as we dropped off and picked up our other children.

Tina and I became friends very quickly and are still great friends to this day. When we used to stand in the playground, I would ask many questions about Amy and Down syndrome. It's the best way to learn and I thought because we had become friends, I wanted to know about her.

The conversation that stands out the most for me was when I asked Tina what it was like when receiving the diagnosis of Down syndrome. Before she began, she said even with the emotions they went through, they loved Amy with all their heart and did from the second she was born.

She told me that when they received the news it was devastating and an extremely emotional time. They had just welcomed their little girl into the world and then had received the news that turned their life upside down. The path they were heading toward had suddenly been changed quite dramatically.

She said there were many tears from them, and their families and it took quite some time to get over those emotions. Those words came back to me in 2005 when I was pregnant with Darcy, and we were having the scans around the 12-week mark of my pregnancy.

Darcy, Aged 17 Years

While having my first scan, the person doing it kept measuring the back of my baby's neck. I knew this was a marker for Down syndrome because of the conversations I'd had with Tina. My mind was racing as I watched, knowing what he was doing. My heart was racing but I had to ask the question.

When I asked him if he thought this was the case, he said he couldn't tell me, and he was only checking his measurements because of how high they were. He told me that if the measurement is over 3mm, there is a strong chance the baby will have Down syndrome. He said the measurements of my baby's neck were 2.8–2.9mm so he just wanted to be sure he had done it correctly.

When I asked him what he thought I should do, he told me to get a second opinion. Well, that's what I did. At the 15-week mark of my pregnancy I went in for another scan with the obstetrician I'd had for my previous boys. He did the scan and told me that even though the measurement was high, everything else looked perfect. The only way we would get a 100% diagnosis would be with an amniocentesis.

He told me if I wanted to do that, today was a good day to do it because of where my baby was laying. There was a very big clear pocket of fluid where he could do the test. Mick and I had already discussed it and decided we wanted to know, so the amniocentesis was performed.

I did know about the risks involved with an amniocentesis, but I trusted this man and knew he would be extremely careful. Blake was in the room with me and was five at the time. I looked at him with his cute cheeky smile and told him what the doctor was going to do. I told him not to worry and everything would be okay. I often wonder what was going through his mind as he saw the doctor approach me with the huge needle in his hand.

Because my pregnancy was at the 15-week mark, he told me he would rush the results through and could get a result as soon as the next day. I told him he didn't need to rush because the results wouldn't make any difference to progressing with the pregnancy.

He was true to his word and we received the results the next day. I remember that day clearly when the phone rang. We were at my mother-in-law's wake surrounded by family and friends. I had a gut feeling that when I answered the phone, he was going to tell me my baby had Down syndrome but when he spoke the words, it was still quite a shock.

This doctor, who had always been very strong in his nature, dry and matter of fact, had a trembling in his voice as he told me the news. He was so sorry and kept repeating that over and over again. I found myself telling him it was going to be okay and please stop saying sorry.

It was an interesting conversation that ended quickly because of where I was at the time. I found Mick and looked at him. I didn't need to say anything as I looked at him, and we both started to cry. I don't know why we cried, because we were expecting him to tell us our baby had Down syndrome. Maybe it was just hearing the words or the relief of knowing. I'm not really sure.

As we headed back into the room where our family and friends were, we decided not to tell anyone because there was enough for everyone to deal with grieving my mother-in-law.

Darcy, Aged 17 Years

Our decision to find out the diagnosis during the pregnancy was because we wanted Darcy to be born into the world the same way as his brothers. We didn't want people being sad the moment he was born, and we wanted his brothers to know so they could ask questions and learn as much as they could.

The boys knew Tina and her family and the only question they had while I was pregnant was, 'Does that mean our brother will be like Amy?' I told them he will have Down syndrome like she does, but he will be different just like we are all different.

It was a good time for everyone to deal with the emotions they would feel when hearing the news. We weren't ready for the reactions from people when we did tell them. I mentioned earlier that we decided not to tell anyone at the wake, but that didn't work.

The news spread fast, and people started coming up to me and throwing themselves on me with a huge embrace and a lot of emotions. It was quite difficult to deal with and when we got home that day, we did question if what we were doing was the right thing. Those thoughts quickly left as we looked at my belly and the movement of the little baby that was going to join our family.

Receiving the diagnosis while pregnant also allowed us to be able to tackle the emotional rollercoaster that comes with the diagnosis. We were able to research and learn as much as we could before our little man was born, or at least try to.

We were also able to join a support/coffee group run by my friend Tina which was amazing. Because we were friends, I knew she ran this group, but I never thought I would end up being part of it.

It was great because we could meet other families and see how their children were progressing. We were able to ask all the questions we had listed and were able to see how the children interacted with everyone and each other.

This was not only great for us as a family, but also wonderful for our parents to see. They could see that our son, when he arrived and began to grow, would interact with friends just as his brothers did. It also allowed everyone to ask us questions before he was born, just as I had done with Tina.

Receiving the diagnosis while pregnant was great for us because we were able to learn as much as we could knowing that our son would be his own person and different from others living with Down syndrome, but it was good to learn the important facts. We also went through the emotions before he was born and there were many of those moments.

Planning things that I learned he would need was great and I was able to make his first appointments with his paediatrician and book him in for early intervention. There was a long waiting list for this, but because I was able to put his name down while I was pregnant, he was able to start this therapy service at one month.

The emotions of others was something we were not quite expecting or ready for and we found ourselves reassuring everyone that things would be fine. Our son would be alright even with a diagnosis of Down syndrome and the additional things we would be doing with him.

We experienced lots of sorrow from our family and friends, but I guess it's because it's the unknown and they didn't know how

Darcy, Aged 17 Years

else to react. Tears and lots of 'I'm sorry' were received from others and we always found ourselves reassuring them everything was going to be alright. Even though we were still unsure, this is what we told people. After all, we were going to have a baby and that's something to be very joyful about no matter what was going to come with him.

We shared our pregnancy journey with everyone that was close to us and also shared all the things we were learning about what our journey may look like in those early years. We did this so they would be able to start learning about Down syndrome and what our lives were possibly going to look like. We could never be 100% certain before he was born because everyone is different.

The reasoning behind receiving the diagnosis prenatally was so that everyone would accept our baby into the world just as they had done with his brothers, and by the time Darcy was born, everyone was so excited to meet him. All the worry had subsided, apart from the general worry we all go through with our children.

There were no tears or sadness when he entered the world. There was lots of love, happiness and great support from everyone in our family as well as our friends. It was exactly how we wanted it to be.

The medical professionals were another story when receiving the diagnosis, and something I wasn't ready for. To be honest, it was extremely hard to deal with.

I understood they needed to tell me my options and I sat listening to them when they described what would happen if I decided to terminate. I didn't like what they told me and found myself very distressed by it.

They told me I would be given a pill that would bring on labour, and I would give birth to my son. Because the pregnancy was so early, my son would die, and we would then have to arrange a funeral and deal with all of those emotions.

I remember going home after listening to this very upset. I cradled my baby bump extra tight each time they told me about this, and each day and night I would tell my little man that was not going to happen.

The subsequent appointments were where they continued to tell me of this termination option even though I had explained we were not going down that route and the reason we wanted the diagnosis at that stage was so we could tell family and friends and we could all gain knowledge about Down syndrome (as much as we could) before he was born.

I was seeing two doctors at the time and by the fifth appointment I was so angry that they kept telling me about termination, I remember yelling saying, 'PLEASE STOP TELLING ME ABOUT THIS.' From then on, thankfully they stopped talking about termination and concentrated on the pregnancy and my baby.

I still to this day don't understand why they felt the need to continually tell me about this option, especially as I had told them we were not going down that road. When I think back, it's almost as though they were trying to bully me into making that decision. For them, it seemed, it was the logical option. But why? I will never know.

I recently saw a quote on social media about the way the news of Down syndrome should be relayed to parents. Most of my friends experienced negativity when receiving the diagnosis and it shouldn't be that way. Yes, they need to be factual and advise of options, but they also need to be caring and remember that our child is a person just like everyone else.

This is the quote:

> *Down syndrome is a naturally occurring chromosome*
> *Arrangement that has always been part of the human condition.*
> *…naturally occurring.*
> *Not an abnormality.*
> *Not a disorder.*
> *Not 'What's wrong with her?'*
> *Can you imagine a doctor walking in and saying,*
> *'Your baby has Down syndrome. Don't worry though.*
> *Children have been born with Down syndrome since the beginning of time.*
> *Down syndrome is a naturally occurring chromosome arrangement*
> *That has always been part of the human condition.*
> *Your child will be blessed to be a member of an amazing population of people that make this world a better place to live in.'*
> *Something as simple as language we could use to change the*
> *Perception of how the world views my child and so many other children.*
> *What a wonderful, wonderful world it would be.*
> **Rose Mardi**

Many years later, when Darcy was around seven, we bumped into one of those doctors. He stopped to say hello and commented about how well Darcy looked and asked how he was going. Once I finished telling him, he said he had something to tell me. He said his nephew, who he is very close with, now has a little girl with Down syndrome. I congratulated him and that was when he told me something that really filled my heart. He told me he got it now, and he understood. Nothing else was needed to be said and we both left that conversation with huge smiles on our faces.

I was happy he felt this way and was experiencing the world of Down syndrome in a positive way, but I wondered how many people his earlier words were heard by. How many people chose termination because of what he told them.

Everyone is different and I never judge anyone for the decisions they make for their families. Never ever would I do that. But I do wonder how many families were bullied into making a decision like termination because of what their doctors told them.

THE VOICE

There is a voice inside of you
That whispers all day long.
'I feel that this is right for me.
I know that this is wrong.'
No teacher, preacher, parent, friend
Or wise man can decide
What's right for you – just listen to
The voice that speaks inside.

Shel Silverstein

For me, the other wonderful thing about receiving the diagnosis while pregnant was that I could get in touch with support early to help us through and teach us about Down syndrome. I got in touch with Down Syndrome Victoria and as mentioned earlier, began attending my friend's support group.

The support group was amazing because I was able to meet other mums and hear their stories as well as meet their children and see how they interacted with everyone. The children were aged between one and seven, and with these families, I found myself beginning to plan my baby's early years even before he was born.

I got to hear about early intervention, medical interventions some had to take, kindergarten years, schooling and about how they all dealt with other things as families. I was able to ask lots of questions without feeling nervous about it. They welcomed any question I had and always answered them with love and honesty. It was wonderful and I loved meeting up every fortnight with these ladies.

Support is so important, and I feel it's equally important to be around like-minded people travelling along the same road you are. It's much like a first mums' group you go to at your local Maternal and Child Health Centre when you are a first-time mum.

You get to bounce stories off each other and listen to different strategies people are using that may also work for you. You've all entered the same journey together and it's great to be able to get this support rather than just sit at home on your own wondering about certain things.

The early years of Darcy's life began with a three-week stay in the special care nursery at the hospital and when he came home, we were able to begin early intervention immediately because I had put him on the waiting list while pregnant, so a spot came up for him as soon as he came home.

This is where I learned about physiotherapy, occupational therapy and speech therapy and how beneficial these would be for my son now and as he continued to grow. It was going to be a busy time for a number of years but something he needed and time to learn for all of us.

Being with the support group and listening to other's experiences, I was also able to begin mapping out Darcy's early educational years and hope that what I was planning would come true. Hoping we would at least be able to try. I've always been a forward thinker and try to plan for what may lay ahead. It doesn't always work but feeling prepared is something I like to do.

When he was a few months old he became very sick, and we discovered he was aspirating his feeds. So, some of the feeds were going into his belly but a lot of it was going onto his lungs.

It explained why his breathing was different and why he was only gaining weight slowly. It was a very scary time and at one point we thought we would lose our beautiful boy.

The medical team we were under throughout this time were simply amazing and so supportive. There were so many new terms we had no idea about and much to learn about the intervention that was needed to help our boy. It was an extremely scary time of months in and out of hospital trying to determine what the best course of action to take was.

I remember one day while sitting in the hospital with Darcy, the Nursing Unit Manager came into our room and sat down. She told me she was there to answer the question I was too scared to ask. I actually had no idea what she was talking about to begin with. However, as she kept talking, I realised there was a big question on my mind, but I had tucked it away because I was scared.

So, she said she will answer it for me. Her words were so strong as she said, **'He's not going to die. He is going to be alright.'** My first reaction was shock, and then I felt relief that she had answered my unspoken question. She was an amazing lady and was such a great support for us during this time. We felt very well looked after and knew that in time, Darcy would be alright.

After many appointments, tests and examinations as well as spending months in and out of hospital, Darcy ended up having a PEG inserted so I could give him his formula and water through the PEG which went straight into his stomach, therefore bypassing the swallowing. When we first went into hospital, it was recommended we put him on solids immediately so he wouldn't lose the ability to chew and swallow and we hoped that one day in the future he may lose the PEG and be independent with drinking.

This was a scary time too because I didn't really have any idea about what this PEG was and how long he may need to have it. It could be a lifelong thing and at the time, that is what we thought it would be. It helped to save his life because it stopped the aspiration dead in its tracks.

Once the PEG was sorted, his lungs were clear, and we got used to life with it, Darcy went through early intervention very well and when it was time, we enrolled him at our local Special Developmental School. He started the EEPS program when he was two years and nine months old and enjoyed a wonderful first year of education.

Other therapies we began for Darcy in his early years were speech and occupational therapy. We had to apply for funding for these as the NDIS was non-existent then, and we were able to enjoy 10 weeks of speech therapy one year followed by 10 weeks of OT the following year. We continued to do this until the NDIS came into effect and now, we are able to attend regular therapy sessions ongoing.

The next two years he would spend in the EEPS program, and he also attended the local mainstream kindergarten his brothers attended. It was so special for him to be able to experience the same things his brothers did, and it was truly wonderful to be able to do both.

We did fundraising to hire an assistant for him in three-year-old kinder, and for four-year-old kinder we enrolled him without asking for an assistant. We did this because there were two other children in the group with additional needs and after discussions with the kinder teacher, we knew there would be ample support for all the children in the group including Darcy. The kinder also had a wonderful volunteer who assisted with all the kids.

Following very successful years in kinder, he began dual schooling. Dual schooling means he attended the special developmental school four days a week and our local mainstream primary school that his brothers attended one day a week.

We were never sure how long this would last for him but wanted to at least try so again, he could experience the same things as his brothers and experience school in a different way to the specialist school.

Darcy took very well to the mainstream setting and stayed at this school for the whole seven years. He attended all the incursions, excursions, specialty days, camps and was part of the Year 6 production as well as graduating with his peers.

We had our fair share of advocating during these years but thankfully, Darcy was able to enjoy the same things as everyone else and we have the best memories to keep forever. There was not a dry eye in the house on the night of graduation – everyone was so proud of him.

Darcy is now 17 years old and is full time at the special developmental school. The high school transition went very well for us with him because he was already at the school so there was no real change apart from new teachers and new classmates, like all students experience.

We decided not to do any mainstream schooling for his secondary years as we felt the gap in age would be too far and difficult to deal with. We did approach a couple of local secondary schools and they told us we would not be eligible for funding even for one day. So, he would not always have an assistant with him. This helped to make the decision and he is very happy in the specialist setting. It is an amazing school, and we are blessed to be able to send Darcy there.

We caught up with one of his primary school friends and he told me he was sad that Darcy didn't come to high school with them all. He said Darcy would have been so good at making new friends. Without an assistant with him for the time required, I just couldn't see it working.

He is a very active young man enjoying basketball with Special Olympics, tenpin bowling and dance. He has recently started doing drama with his dance group and he loves acting out certain characters. It's been great for his speech development and one the reasons we enrolled him to attend. He also does love to be a showman and gets into character very quickly.

We have amazing support, and they assist Darcy with all of his activities as well as assisting with his independence skills. They have been instrumental in Darcy achieving a lot of his goals as well as overcoming some fears he had in the community.

He loves to go out and particularly enjoys concerts, the theatre, watching his favourite team South East Melbourne Phoenix at the basketball and going to the football. I love doing these activities with him because of the way he enjoys it. He doesn't worry about who is watching and reacts to what he is watching so naturally. He really enjoys every moment to the fullest.

He is a very funny young man that loves to make people smile. He is kind and looks after his friends and family especially if he can see they are feeling down. It is a beautiful quality he has and it amazes me how much he is in tune to everyone's feelings. Sometimes, if I am feeling down, I try to hide it from him, but he always knows. He will come and put a hand on my shoulder or give me a hug just when I need it. He does this for everyone.

We have always tried to make Darcy's life the same as ours enjoying lots of days out and other fun activities but sometimes it's hard because of others. Other people staring, pointing or making remarks about him.

In the early days I used to always say something to these people, but I found it was making my day very negative and I would always go home quite upset. Now, I've changed the way I respond and try very hard to ignore what I see.

It's very hard to do because I wonder why people feel the need to make comments or stare at my son the way they do. It's very uncomfortable. I find myself getting very angry when comments are made because I don't understand why they feel the need to do it. My son is not going home with them, and they don't have to look after him.

The feelings you get when people are being judgemental are very overwhelming and cause a lot of anxiety especially when they say something nasty. I really don't understand why they think it's okay to say something and pass judgement on my son. I honestly don't know how we can change this either and that makes me sad for Darcy.

I know, with the stares, not everyone is staring in a negative way, but for me and because Darcy has Down syndrome, I perceive it as negative immediately. Over the years I've changed the way I deal with this, and I now give people a smile, wave or even say hello. Most people respond in a positive way which is awesome and does show that not all stares are negative.

It's important to us and for Darcy, that he be treated as a person. His disability is a visual one and sometimes he is treated according to that rather than the person who he is. Please see him for who he is – a young man with dreams and aspirations like everyone else.

Down syndrome is a big part of him, but it is not all of him. It plays a big part in who he is and how he learns, but he is a person before anything else and there are many wonderful sides to our boy.

It's important for people to be kind, inclusive and accepting because everyone deserves a chance to be part of something. To experience life like everyone else. To feel as though they are part of a community and to feel as though they can have a go if they want to.

Feeling excluded is not a nice feeling and it can happen even when you just go to the shop, catch a bus, go for a walk and any other things you may want to do. It makes you feel as though you shouldn't do it and causes a lot of loneliness for some.

One of my favourite things about Darcy is his ability to see people for who they are and not worry about what they look like or if they behave a little differently. He takes people for exactly how he sees them and is inclusive and accepting of them all. He will talk and interact with everyone but if they are unkind to him, he will stop. That is the only thing that will stop him and nothing else.

Wouldn't it be great to see the world through my son's eyes and accept everyone for who they are.

Give People A Chance And Watch Them Shine
Julie Fisher

Follow Julie, Darcy and their family here:

The Unexpected Journey - https://www.facebook.com/theunexpectedjourneybook
Discovering Darcy - https://www.facebook.com/discoverdarcy
Instagram - https://www.instagram.com/juliefisher183_author/

Darcy, Aged 17 Years

ERIN AND DIANE
Chicago, Illinois, USA

Erin, Aged 17 Years

When I was pregnant with Erin, we found out that she had a high probability of having Down syndrome during our 20-week scan.

It was interesting because the screening tests we had with Ryan, my first-born son, showed he too, had an increased risk for Down syndrome. We had an amniocentesis for my son because we were so scared and spent a very anxious month of his pregnancy worrying, only to find out he was genetically typical.

So, for Megan, our second-born daughter, we decided we were not going to do any testing because it was such a terrible experience, putting us through the emotions of having a child with Down syndrome without actually having a child with Down syndrome.

With Erin, we wanted to avoid testing, too, but we made an appointment for the more diagnostic ultrasound. I even wanted to leave the ultrasound waiting room, but something made me stay. I'm not sure what it was because I knew it didn't matter what may come up. We were always going to have her, but I stayed in the waiting room. It was that decision that saved Erin's life the first time.

In the ultrasound, things were looking fine. All the usual markers for Down syndrome didn't seem to be there. The neck measurements and nose measurements were fine, so it seemed okay.

Towards the end of the appointment, they found her Duodenal Atresia, which is a blockage in the intestine. When the doctor saw this, he decided to look a little closer and found a sparkly heart muscle which evidently is the telltale sign of an AV canal. With

Erin, Aged 17 Years

these findings, the geneticist followed his diagnosis of suspected Down syndrome with the words, 'There's no excuse for a child like this to born in this day and age.' I couldn't believe my ears. I was mortified. I didn't get out of bed for the next three days, I just couldn't. I knew we were not going to terminate, but it was just really hard. The whole time I was in bed, I could feel this little baby kicking and, in my heart, I knew she would be amazing no matter what they said.

At the time there was a well-known US soccer player, Mia Hamm, and our daughter was doing just as much kicking as Mia was. I remember thinking, this baby doesn't know people don't think she is a blessing. She doesn't know there are some terrible things wrong. I decided then I needed to get back up and into the game.

I remember when the doctor told us about her heart, we thought, 'What could possibly be wrong with a sparkly heart muscle?' Now that she is older, I think her personality and everything else has confirmed the sparkly heart muscle diagnosis.

We didn't have an amniocentesis because a Down syndrome diagnosis wouldn't have changed anything about us having her. Plus, amniocentesis can sometimes cause miscarriage, and with her heart condition, we didn't want to risk it. Down syndrome also seemed minor compared to the other conditions.

During the pregnancy, we were monitored as high risk because of Erin's health issues, and finally at around 31 weeks, they told us she was probably going to be premature.

There were some things going on with the placenta. It wasn't holding up very well and I needed to start having steroid shots to help her lungs develop sooner.

During this time, we also encountered a doctor who said our selfish religious beliefs were dooming this child to life as a vegetable, and that God did not make her to survive. He told us if we were truly Christian, we would not seek any treatment. We believed that God also made doctors and sent us the guidance to have treatment, so we decided to get the shots to give her a shot for the best quality of life.

I had to stay in the hospital for 48 hours after the shots and while I was there, the medical team saw that her heart rate was decelerating. That meant I wasn't allowed to leave the hospital. I had to stay for the rest of the pregnancy. Her heart rate kept decelerating, so we ended up having her at 32 weeks.

The doctors kept warning us that the odds of Erin passing away were quite high. We brought her brother, Ryan, and sister, Megan, to the hospital. The nurses worked to find a way they could meet their sister and say good-bye if needed. Ryan and Megan loved Erin already, so the nurses' care meant so much to our family.

My husband told the doctor we did believe in a better place if it looked as though Erin wasn't going to make it. He said just wrap her in a blanket and give her to us to say good-bye.

After Erin was delivered, we saw the medical team working on her, but we didn't hear crying. So, when the doctor wrapped Erin in a blanket and gave her to my husband, we thought our worst fears had come true. The doctor, who knew our little soccer player had just scored amazing on the newborn screening tests, realised our confusion, and said, 'No, no – this is what we do with all the babies who are doing well. We wrap them in a blanket and give them to the parents.' In fact, Erin had APGAR scores higher than Ryan and Megan's. She had an eight when she was born, then she started looking around and scored a nine. The doctor couldn't give her a ten because Erin wouldn't cry. And she didn't cry for several months.

We still had all the other medical conditions to take care of, including having surgery the first day of her life. She was so tiny only weighing three pounds. The doctors told us the surgery would take six to seven hours, so when Greg walked in to my hospital room after three hours I panicked. He told me not to worry, everything was done, and she was fine. She defied the odds once again. Ryan and Megan concentrated on showering her with gifts to make sure she felt welcome. Megan wrote the alphabet and numbers on a piece of cardboard, and announced it was Erin's first computer. I was instructed to show Erin how it worked. Ryan bought her little stuffed animals with gripping hands to decorate the steel bars of the NICU crib so that Erin didn't think she was in jail.

Part of our challenge when she was in the NICU was finding her because she was the most stable baby in there. She was always the baby they were able to move easily when they needed space. I couldn't believe it. I remember thinking how a baby with all these conditions can be the most stable? That was my first lesson in not underestimating her and to respectfully ignore people who were using their personal experiences or professional training to underestimate her.

I learned to listen to allies like the NICU nurse who coached me to 'stay feisty' and keep advocating for Erin. Even more importantly, I learned not to listen to people like the social worker who told me when Erin was four days old that the good news is that we can, 'Keep her when she is cute and little, and then institutionalise her when she gets older and is hard to manage.'

I often say, with Erin we see the best and worst in people – we have had so many cases of where we have preconceived notions of people that end up not being true. This also happens the other way around, when we think someone will be helpful, like the social worker at the hospital or Erin's school administrators, and they are not.

I remember we saw several men on motorcycles at a gas station late at night when we were on vacation. They were staring at us, as people sometimes do when you have a child with a disability. I began preparing all my mama defences, when one of the bigger guys spoke like the cartoon character Donald Duck, which made Erin erupt into laughter. It broke the ice, and we ended up having a lovely conversation with these guys. It was a good lesson that all of us have preconceived notions and biases that don't serve us well, especially as many of us become disability allies for the first time in our lives. We should never judge.

So, it was the same with the doctors. Some came to us with a real clinical point of view that Erin wasn't normal. To them, she was an abnormal genetic deficit, who wasn't worthy of medical care. Several doctors seemed more concerned about their duty to spare the rest of world from the expense and bother of caring for her. One of these doctors was concerned for our other children and the harm they would have from having Erin as a sister. Another doctor wanted to put then six month old Erin through a complicated surgery and 10 days of hospitalisation to insert a feeding tube because 'it would be easier to feed her in the institution,' as staff wouldn't have to take the time to feed her by hand.

But we also had many doctors who were just lovely. One told us he knew several people with Down syndrome as adults and they're fabulous people who lead great lives. We were relieved when he came in off-shift to deliver Erin, bringing his positive attitude with him. A second, the cardiologist who treated Erin's 'sparkly heart muscle,' definitely had a fabulous heart of her own, as she guided us through the initial shock of heart surgery and serving as Erin's first medical advocate by issuing a formal complaint on our behalf against the geneticist who had diagnosed Erin so terribly.

This cardiologist was good for our hearts as well as Erin's. As was Erin's paediatrician, Dr Peggy Supple. She was the only paediatrician out of 26 in our insurance plan, who was willing to take Erin on as a patient. She stood by us every step of the way. Often calling us at midnight when Erin was sick because she was just as worried as we were (and knew we would be awake but wouldn't want to bother her). She got Erin through a pandemic, quarantining her home two weeks before official lockdowns started because she had been watching the pandemic in other countries and was concerned, saying she had worked too hard to lose our girl to a virus.

Doctors must understand that just like an ultrasound can't be used to figure out who's going to be a baseball star, or who's going to be a soccer or football star, it also can't be used to predict the future of kids with disabilities. The ultrasound is medical equipment not a fortune telling machine.

We need to know the truth about our children's conditions and diagnosis, but we also need to be told of positive stories and successes. It would make the experience a lot easier to deal with at the time. We need to be told all the options. It's a legal and ethical thing they need to do, but they need to add the supports and positives.

Now that Erin is grown and 17, I would much rather the human race be more like her. If they were, a lot more people would change the way they enjoy life. Erin has no judgement and takes everyone as she sees them.

Erin and I are working on a book chapter now and one of the things she says, which I love, is that we shouldn't limit communication to just talking. She said there are many ways to communicate. I totally agree with her. Why should we limit communication to just one way when there are so many options out there?

When Erin was born, our family and friends were very supportive. We had so many medical things going on, and she was in hospital for 58 days after she arrived. She had two surgeries immediately and then needed another at six months of age for her heart. We had to stay in quarantine after the surgery, so for us, going into lockdown with Covid wasn't so unusual. It has been a way of life for us from time to time. My mum, who thankfully was a nurse practitioner, moved in, helping ensure Ryan and Megan could live their best lives, as well as become very close with their gramma and grampa. She also became the in-house medical expert.

After Erin's surgery, we couldn't see people under instructions from her cardiologist. She said there were no visitors allowed in our home, and we had to shower and launder clothes immediately upon arrival. I jokingly asked if we could hold her up to the front window for people to stand in our front yard and see her—the home version of the NICU window, and the doctor actually said that was a good idea.

During this time, I relied a lot on my son. Erin had an NG feeding tube for about a year. She was an absolute master of yanking the tube out. Many years later, occupational therapists would comment on Erin's amazing fine motor skills, which we credited to her self-initiated NG tube removal exercises. Big brother Ryan would help stand watch, trying to keep her hands busy and away from the tube. He also would help hold and comfort her while we put it back in after she inevitably succeeded in pulling it out, smiling, and handing it to us in victory. Eventually, she learned to eat by mouth, and we could say goodbye to the NG tube.

Once we got through the first year, we knew there was going to be a lot of hospitalisations for Erin, as she probably spent at least half of her first year in hospital. The second year of her life we called 'sniper fire'. Everything would be going along fine and then, BOOM! We were back in the hospital.

I always tried to keep her out of hospital, but I had to change that mindset. If she was having trouble staying hydrated, I would spoon feed her water one tablespoon each hour. It would all go well and then all of a sudden, she would throw everything up and we would have to get her straight to hospital.

She would then begin to crash, which meant doctors couldn't find a vein to start an IV, and she would end up hospitalised for days. I had to change my mindset that the hospital was not a bad place to be avoided, but a place that we could go to for help and health. If we get her straight in, dehydration could be handled very easily, and we would probably be home in a couple of hours not days.

It's all very logical now, but at the time, I just wanted to keep her out of hospital. I was really fighting to keep her home. This is why the metaphor of 'fighting for health' isn't always helpful. While we all want great health, medical issues aren't the enemy.

I had to accept that it was something we needed for her at the time. Get her to the hospital quickly so they can give her fluids and send us home rather than waiting and ending up in hospital for days, sometimes having the airlift crew come to find a vein. If they couldn't get one in her arm or anywhere else, they would have to put the IVs in her head. Erin and I didn't like that at all.

Changing my mindset of what was bad is now good took a while, but I think it's something most mums in the same position would go through.

When Erin finally made it home from the NICU, she was on oxygen. It was such a scary time and probably our lowest moment. I remember the oxygen monitor going off in the middle of the night. My brain would be alert and telling me to get the baby, but the memo would not have gone to my legs. So, I would come rolling out of bed and fall to the floor clamouring, now and again.

The other scary thing at home was giving her the medication. In the NICU, it would be two nurses monitoring her and then administering. But at home, it was just me. I would have to listen to her heart, take her pulse and keep in mind, this was the middle of the night I'm talking about.

So, I had my watch, and I would start counting, but all of a sudden, I realised I was saying '375, 376' because I just kept counting past the minute pulse-taking time, as I was so tired. Initially I would laugh, but then I would start crying, wondering how I was supposed to do this for her.

People go through a lot of training to do this professionally, and here I was at 3am without any more than two hours sleep at a time for weeks, trying to monitor her and give her medication. But you keep going because you have got to do what you have got to do.

Supports for us were difficult locally. When I called one support group, which incidentally was after I counted to 376, a lady and I talked for a while, but then she told me that a child like Erin, with all these physical things going on, will most likely be low functioning. It was very frustrating because she didn't know. She had never met my daughter, but that didn't stop her from stereotyping. It felt like a pity party. That didn't sit well with me. I had the mindset that I would make the best of everything and so would Erin. If she had greater support needs, we would figure that out.

A lot of people said I was in denial, but I found denial a very strong coping mechanism. I was so busy trying to get through the physical stuff that even when the representative told me Erin would be low functioning, I told myself I just had to keep her alive, take her next pulse, and hope we could get to a time in the future when support levels mattered. I didn't know if that was even a possibility or a stretch of a goal, but it was a mindset that kept me focused.

When Erin was three, we did start a literacy program through Gigi's Playhouse. It's a nationwide group and it was fantastic. The parents I met there were very much like me in wanting to seek answers and they were also looking for the positives. We were all asking, 'What do we do to move forward?' And we didn't even think our children wouldn't read, of course they would. Some of the people we met there are still my friends today.

Sometimes we try different support groups, and they don't fit with us, so it's just a matter of finding the right one that fits with your family at that particular time, and for that particular need.

I really saw the differences in all the kids too, so if you think all kids with Down syndrome are the same, they're not. Erin and her best friend couldn't be more different, but they fit.

Online support is good, too, and a lot of people are using that now, especially with Covid and all the lockdowns. It's also great online because you can connect with people all over the world, hear their stories and support each other that way. Now we have been exposed to the online world, we can access both online and face-to-face support and classes.

Some of the therapy we do is also a great support. With Erin's physical conditions, we accessed whatever therapy we could. At one year of age, she had the physical skills of a newborn. Some of the surgeries halted her milestones. For example, she was able to sit up, but when she had the heart surgery and the doctor cut her collarbone and sternum, it set her back a lot.

We had early intervention, which provided therapists who came to the house. Because of surgery at six months and healing time, we didn't start until Erin was nine months old. The physical therapist came and noticed we were still holding Erin's head up, as you do with a newborn. Erin had had extensive heart surgery, after all, so we were still in protection mode. The physical therapist sat us down and told us Erin was in charge of her own head. She pointed out that Erin's head was still shaky like a bobble head toy, because we weren't giving her a chance to develop her strength.

She concluded the lecture by saying we were bobble head enablers. We had very good intentions, but we were over-helping and not giving Erin dignity of risk – meaning we were protecting her to the point of stifling her development. After that lecture,

Erin, Aged 17 Years

big sister Megan had made a stadium seat cushion out of foam with a strap for easy carrying in Girl Scouts. Our cushion never made it to a sporting event, as it became the sport itself.

Megan would place Erin on her tummy, propped up on elbows, and then use the strap to pull her around the house, working up to a full run. It was a bit scary to watch, but Erin would laugh and laugh. When the physical therapist saw this, she promoted Megan to Physical Therapy Assistant, and said that was a fabulous developmental activity. Ever since, I have used the term, bobble head enabler, to ensure I am providing Erin opportunities to grow and live her best life. When faced with decisions like going on a sleepover or learning challenging subjects at school, I ask myself, 'Am I being a bobble head enabler?'

When we do find a therapist or medical professional who understands and is a true helper, we work to keep the relationship lifelong. For example, the early intervention speech therapist who helped Erin until she was three years old, we were able to continue to see her through private insurance. She ended up moving to another state and becoming a professor at a university's speech pathology department. During the pandemic, telemedicine became acceptable, and Erin was able to begin working with her and her students, improving her articulation and helping her use speech to text tools more easily.

Swim therapy was another early intervention therapy we used. Erin actually learned to walk at age three at swim therapy because the water helped to hold her up. The therapist used a platform submerged in the pool, with the support of the water helping Erin walk long before she was able to on land. It gave her lots of skills and muscle development. After that, she would take a rest in the car, while we drove to a physical therapist for another hour of therapy on land. We called it Surf and Turf Therapy Day.

That therapist used the toys Erin enjoyed, making therapy fun. When my sister-in-law sent Erin a dance ribbon one Christmas, Erin immediately took to it, spinning it for hours. Seeing that interest, the therapist asked us to bring the ribbon, and she used it for strengthening exercises. Big sister Megan, who was a dancer, worked hard to learn rhythmic gymnastics, and became Erin's first coach. Erin now participates in rhythmic gymnastics for Special Olympics.

Music therapy was something Erin really loved, so when early intervention was over, we joined a children's music class. Erin did that until she was about six or seven, and it's where she learned to gallop. She would see the other children doing it and wanted to do it too. It really is about finding a child's talents, interests and dreams, no matter their abilities or age, and helping them grow.

Sign language was something we used when she was young, with Erin telling people that American Sign Language was her first language. The benefit of it was she was able to develop age-appropriate vocabulary even though she couldn't speak at the time.

Even when she did begin to learn words and speak verbally, she would go back to ASL to help organise her thoughts. We also use ASL to help learn and memorise information for tests. The ASL provides a kinetic way of learning. She even did the preamble for the constitution in sign, and it was really helpful for her.

The only downfall with the therapy was the cost. Erin was born at the time when they were beginning to make cuts. So, there were people there having the therapy funded and then there was us who didn't qualify because of the funding cuts that were being made.

We were deemed as middle class which didn't help, and the swim therapy was $300 an hour so we could only really afford one hour class a month. Erin was thriving with it, but we just couldn't have her do more because of the cost and eventually we had to stop all together.

Our state has a lot of issues and is one of the last states that still uses state-operated institutions to house people with intellectual disabilities. While Erin has been on a waiting list for almost 15 years for services that would help with her care, institutions are considered to be an entitlement, meaning that if we decided we couldn't look after Erin anymore, we could always institutionalise her.

I can't get services to help her in the home, but I can call and get her put into an institution. It is a little harder to find a spot now because Covid has caused staffing shortages, which means families who have high support needs have to make really hard choices.

Even a child like Erin could be put into an institution just because we, as her parents, said so. Erin is very determined and has achieved so much. She has been successful at many things, and we would still be able to choose to send her to an institution.

Erin sees herself as an advocate, and I think this is because of the many things she has been through and the people who have mentored her. One of those people is Cindy Montgomery from TeachAbility. When you ask Erin what job she wants to do, she will tell you that she wants to be President of the United States. A lot of people hear that goal and either laugh, or worse, launch into a lecture about why that is an impossible goal to achieve.

However, Cindy heard Erin's goal and said, 'Okay, this is something I can work with,' and began listing the skills she would need, like participating in meetings and researching laws. Cindy recruited Erin to be a member of the State Rehabilitation Council, not only giving Erin government experience, but ensuring the Council hears real-life information that will help them inform their decisions. Cindy is now coaching Erin on becoming the secretary of the Council, so that she will get note taking experience, and have a chance to be on the Executive Committee.

Erin wants to make a difference in the world, but there are a lot of people who don't see that as a good thing, especially at her high school. It is hard to change a system when there is a power imbalance. Studies show that standardised tests are often not an accurate measure of performance for students with Down syndrome, yet schools tend to rely on them. In Erin's case, she has expressive language issues, so while she knows a lot and has complex thoughts, trying to get those thoughts out on paper or in speech can be a challenge.

Because of that, testing showed that Erin was scoring as a first or second grader, which the school used to justify teaching her at a first or second grade level. Follow-up testing would then show Erin hadn't learned the information the school hadn't taught her, with Erin still scoring at the first or second grade level. However, when accommodations are used, the school's testing shows that Erin scores at grade level in reading and writing.

Erin, Aged 17 Years

During the Covid lockdowns, Erin did really well with virtual school. Because of immune system issues, Erin has missed a lot of school over the years, sometimes even whole semesters. During one and half years of lockdown, Erin missed three days in total. When Erin discovered she could have a life without being sick all the time, especially with Covid ramping up to an all-time high when students returned to in-person school, she asked to keep going to virtual school. The school were not keen on this, but Erin and I have been very strong with advocating for her benefit.

At the moment I am advocating for her to school at home. It is the most restrictive to some, but in Erin's case, the most restrictive is hospital. If we can keep her out of there, that's a good thing and what we all want.

I'm not really sure why I'm having to fight for this, because the school were not including her anyway, so if we did send her back, she would be in a self-contained class being taught first and second grade instead of 10th grade material. With virtual school during the lockdowns, she was learning some amazing things and understanding it all. At school, they will take her back to a lower level.

As parents and educators, we need to be careful to not turn a learning disability into an educational disadvantage. That's not right as far as I am concerned and it's not fair on our kids.

Erin loves so many things and learning is one of the things that is at the top of the list. She loves history, so she googled one day and found there was a re-enactment at Gettysburg, Pennsylvania. It was the first week of quarantine and she really wanted to go.

Of course, with all the lockdowns during Covid, it was cancelled for two years. When things opened up again, we went to New York to visit my brother and on our way back, low and behold, the re-enactment was planned for the day after we left.

Of course, we had to stay so Erin could experience this as she had been looking forward to it for so long. We sent our other daughter home on a plane, and we spent an extra couple of days so we could attend. She thoroughly enjoyed it and loves hands on learning, so it was well worth staying on.

In addition to rhythmic gymnastics, Erin takes ballet lessons at the prestigious Joffrey Ballet in Chicago. Joffrey being inclusive means so very much to Erin and our family. They have an adaptive program which has been perfect for Erin. This was done online with classes during the last couple of years, allowing her to do what she loved, and breaking the boredom of being at home.

Erin does both inclusive and integrated dance, which are different, but equally amazing. Inclusive dance is with dancers of all abilities performing together, using a traditional dance format. The ability level of the dance is lowered, so it is accessible for everyone.

Integrated dance starts with the person and then builds the dance from what they can do.

Technically, the dance could not be done without the disability. The pieces that come from this are spectacular, as dancers build and combine choreographic phrases meaningful to them.

Erin recently had her first professional show, called, 'Unfolding Disability Futures', created by Sydney Erlikh and Maggie Bridger.

Erin, Aged 17 Years

It was just beautiful. The theme of Erin's dance was disability mentoring and art was imitating life as Erin was dancing with her dance mentors. We were seeing Erin's future unfold right before our eyes. It was amazing and full of so much goodness.

She also does a program called 'The Young Choreographers Project' out of Los Angeles. Again, with this during Covid, we were able to attend via Zoom. She's now participating in a version that partners a choreographer with a young composer. Erin is using the program to design her own level four rhythmic gymnastics routine with customised music written specifically for it. It is incredible when all the pieces come together.

Erin is basing her piece on the civil war because that is something she is extremely interested in. The young composer did an amazing job of creating modern civil war music.

We are so grateful for the positive people in Erin's life and the opportunities they have given her. The guidance and support to make sure she has a chance to participate in the things she loves is wonderful.

When I was pregnant with Erin, I had received a grant from the state to teach technology to kids at risk. I had students with behavioural issues as well as developmental disabilities.

I went to the high school I thought Erin would attend and met a young man named Daniel who was a powerful self-advocate. He told me he wanted to be a journalist and so we began working on goals to make that happen. We did script writing, video and editing. Daniel had a significant stutter and other challenges, but you knew when he said he wanted to do something, he would.

I was meeting all these people who self-advocated and I saw what they did and how they did it to ensure they lived their best lives and achieved their dreams. When we found out Erin would have issues, I was able to take what I learned from Daniel and some of the other students I met and model that for Erin.

Daniel ended up launching a podcast called 'Special Chronicles Podcast' at a time when podcasts were still very new. It was wonderful to watch it all unfold. Together we had devised this idea of full circle inclusion, which is the right and ability to dream and then make those dreams come true.

Everyone should be allowed to dream and work towards making them come true. Don't put people in a box because of their disability and tell them the job they will be doing, especially if that's not what they want to do. Everyone should be able to at least learn and try to do what they are wanting to do.

It was great watching Daniel, and we really thought Erin would do well at this school because of all the wonderful things we were seeing Daniel achieve. Unfortunately, it just has not turned out like that. The special ed director we thought would be supportive, didn't end up being that way for Erin. The door shut.

The school was not willing to help Erin achieve her goals, and it was extremely frustrating. What I have realised is that when there is a minority group, the people in the minority can't be the ones to change the mindset of those in the majority. The mindset change must be initiated by the people in control, in power. Until we get that mindset changed, there really isn't much that people with disabilities can do to help pull change through. That has been eye-opening for me. I've done a lot of research and gone to Partners in Policy Making which is a program designed to teach parents how to advocate, but none of it mattered. The school was determined to not provide Erin an education. I couldn't make that change for Erin and it really hurt.

The sad thing, especially here in Illinois where we have several institutions is that if someone like Erin comes out with a limited first grade education, she will have so many less opportunities than if the school had accommodated her disability and educated her.

The institution costs are $160,000–$190,000 per year per person and from that, people get $60 per month. So, the people of Illinois can't afford that system or the mindset of segregation. We know that segregated classes lead to segregated communities, and we just can't afford that. It's not a doable option and so important for parents to advocate.

This is where we really need to come together for inclusion and acceptance. I have heard some people with children with disabilities say their children can't handle inclusion, showing that inclusion is a mindset not a place, and it has to be what is best for each person. If you throw a student with disabilities into a general education classroom without support, there is going to be disaster.

Everyone needs some type of support, and if we work together and provide those necessary supports, then good things will happen. Everyone is given tools and support during their lives with school, work and many other things. So, for me, it's just what needs to happen.

Helping people to achieve their dreams is so important. Like when Erin said she wanted to be President, but the school said it was an unachievable goal. I don't know why they didn't say they could get her involved in student government or get her involved in a debate team. She didn't get any type of support with that dream. No goal setting, no tips, or alternatives, just 'that's unachievable'.

I wish the disability community could work together more. I think sometimes we get in our own little silos and forget that everyone is different. Not working together really hurts everyone.

In our country, people with disabilities are the largest minority group, so we could really make some great changes if we all just came together and saw the bigger picture.

It's the mindset, the expensive segregation mindset. If we could just get rid of that medical model of disability that says these kids need to be separated and taken care of, it would make such a difference. The segregation is not sustainable. I feel like a bit of a radical sometimes asking that we all come together and make change.

I want people to understand that Erin is a teenage girl, figuring out who she is. Others don't know better than her because they are not her. She doesn't have to live up to their expectations or live down to their expectations, either.

Sometimes if things are too much, she will shut down and people will perceive that as if she doesn't like them. She has a disability, and this is her way of just communicating that she needs a minute. You know, like if she's just walked into a room and needs to adjust to her surroundings. I think we all do that sometimes. If people give her that grace and don't write her off immediately, they will be surprised at what she can do.

Erin, Aged 17 Years

I would love people to support those of us trying to make good changes. Sometimes I feel as though things are going well and then something happens and I can see they're not. I would love people to open their hearts and minds and listen to us so we can allow our kids to live their best lives just like everyone else.

It may look different to some, but that's okay. All our lives are different, and those differences should be embraced. It hasn't always been easy, but we are proud to be a family who can do hard things. As Ryan, Erin and Megan build lives of their own, I hope they always remember that.

> *'We know discrimination when we see it,
> and we need to be fighting it together.'*
> ***Judith Heumann***

SAXON AND NARELLE
Frankston, Melbourne, Australia

Saxon, Aged 19 Years

My pregnancy was great with Saxon. I had all of the standard prenatal testing available at the time, and there were no indicators that there was going to be any challenges.

I wanted to try for a natural birth but after 22 hours of labour, they told me things were not progressing and started prepping me for a caesarean. Just as they were wheeling me to the theatre, Saxon decided it was time to make his entrance into the world. So, I was able to proceed with a natural birth after all.

Because he was my first child, I wasn't familiar with babies, and nothing was obvious to me at first. He had all the normal checks by the paediatrician who was at the hospital for the birth. For me, that night in the hospital, everything was normal, and I had no idea that anything was wrong.

During the night, the midwives were coming in and out of my room and when I look back now, I realise there was something going on but at the time I had no idea that it was unusual for him to be sleeping so much, he didn't want to feed, and he wasn't crying.

The next morning the midwives told me they had called in the paediatrician to check him as they felt he was a little unwell. They told me they needed to leave him with minimal contact and left him in his crib. I wasn't allowed to hold him at that stage as he was unwell, and they wanted him to be checked.

Finally, when the afternoon came around, a paediatrician came in. She spent quite a bit of time examining Saxon, sat me down and told me she thought my baby had Down syndrome. She wasn't 100% certain because she said he didn't present with most of the features, and it can't be categorically confirmed until we do the microfiche test or the genetic testing.

On top of that, and more important than his diagnosis, she was concerned about his survival as he was incredibly unwell. We had to move to the ICU at Monash because the hospital we were at was only a regional hospital in Mornington.

She had to prepare him to be helicoptered and it was so traumatic. So much was going on and all I wanted was my baby to be okay. The helicopter took him away and I wasn't allowed to go with him. It wasn't part of the process for the mum to go with the baby, which just shouldn't happen. I should have been able to go with him.

I was left in the hospital by myself overnight hearing all the other babies crying without my baby and not knowing if he was going to survive or not. So, the next morning I checked myself out and went straight to Monash so I could be with Saxon.

He spent the next two weeks in intensive care while they tried to do what they could to get him better. It was such a scary time and when they told me the things that were going on, I was terrified.

He had two cephalohematomas (an accumulation of blood under the scalp), severe jaundice and a blood infection that was unidentified. Three days later he was officially diagnosed with Down syndrome. So much to process and so many questions to ask, but all I was worried about was that he would survive.

There was no option for me to stay with him in the hospital either. I had to keep driving up and back to try and feed and look after him. But even in the ICU, there wasn't any room for the parents. It was a very difficult time, and I was relieved when he was transferred to a local hospital. He went to Frankston

Hospital and spent another couple of weeks there learning to feed before I could bring him home.

It was an extremely tough time but medically, they saved his life and were awesome. The paediatrician we had was incredibly helpful because when we were transferred to Monash, I didn't understand a lot of the language and terminology they were using. I didn't realise that when they said fish, they meant microfiche.

I was given a lot of information from the specialists there but couldn't understand what it all meant. I had to ring the paediatrician and get the specialists to speak with her so she could interpret what was happening to my baby just so I could understand. It was probably due to the shock that I wasn't comprehending everything.

They took me into a room at Monash where they confirmed the diagnosis of Down syndrome and I was offered genetic counselling, but to be honest, the only thing I knew about Down syndrome was that it happened to babies that were born to older women. So, I felt as though it was my fault. I was worried if I went to a genetic counsellor, because of the way they termed it, my husband and his family would blame me for his birth.

So, I rejected all the counselling, but in hindsight, I wish they called it something else as I probably would have taken it up. I refused it because of what it was called, and I found it very confronting.

Medically, all the doctors were great, but I think there were so many things lacking. The fact that I couldn't stay with my baby when I needed to bond with him was really poor. I couldn't hold him when we were at Mornington and then I couldn't stay with him at Monash.

Saxon, Aged 19 Years

There was one specialist at Monash that really upset me. Saxon had two cephalohematomas on his head and they looked like little horns. This specialist came in and said, 'Oh he looks like a warlock.' Now, this was the specialist that had just told me my son had a lifelong disability and when he said that it really upset me. I found it extremely offensive and upsetting and I'll never forget him.

The bedside manner was terrible. I understand that they can't look after the mums because they're trying to save baby's lives, but there was really no care for me at that time. It's the most crucial time for a mother and baby to bond, so there's a real gap there. I don't know what it's like now, but then, the gap in that care was huge.

I had no idea what to expect and the first time I felt comfort was the day we got discharged from Monash. A nurse came up and congratulated me for having Saxon. She actually said congratulations and that was the first time anyone had said anything positive to me. It was three weeks after he was born.

One of the nurses we had when we were at Frankston was amazing and we have become lifelong friends. She said to me, 'Don't ever let anyone tell you that he can't do anything.' She also tried to help me breastfeed and she was very helpful. So, there were these two nurses/midwives that made all the difference to me, and it did help tremendously.

The doctors did what they do best and that is, they saved Saxon's life and of course I am forever grateful and appreciate everything they did. A lot more effort needs to go into everything else including their bedside manner and the care for the mums. I needed comfort and guidance and care, and I didn't receive what I thought they should have been giving me.

Support from family was interesting. My mum was supportive which was great because my mother-in-law was not. She told me that Saxon had Down syndrome because of my side of the family. She was ignorant and blamed me.

My sister-in-law got upset because she was having a baby around the same time, and she felt that Saxon was getting more attention than her baby was. Very strange the way some people react, and I couldn't believe it when she said that to me.

Saxon's dad, my husband at the time, disappeared for two weeks. He couldn't cope with the diagnosis and left us. I didn't know where he went or if he was coming back. I assumed that not only had I just had a baby in these circumstances, but I was also convinced my marriage was over. I was on my own travelling back and forth to the hospital to feed and look after Saxon.

I didn't think he would cope with the diagnosis, but I didn't think he would leave. He just went off the grid and disappeared for two weeks. Apparently, he was at a friend's house and just went to work every day as though we didn't even exist.

It was very isolating, but I did have support and strength around me in my girlfriends. They were absolutely everything to me. They came over, painted my nails, rubbed my arm, and did whatever it was that I needed without me having to ask. I honestly don't think I would have survived without my girlfriends' love and support, and this is still very true today. They are my heroes.

The maternal health nurse gave me the number of a lady called Tina Naughton who was running a coffee/support group for mums with children with Down syndrome in our area. I reached out to Tina and joined the group even though I was quite reluctant at the time. I'm glad I did because I met some lovely ladies that I'm still friends with today. They were the only connection I had for others with kids with Down syndrome.

I did feel a little lost at the start because a lot of the mums had kids that were school age and Saxon was a newborn. They were lovely people, but I did find where they were at with their older children and the challenges they faced very overwhelming. I was frightened because I wasn't anywhere near that stage.

The decisions they were facing with schooling and other things like that was quite difficult for them and I wasn't ready to hear any of that because I was just trying to deal with my baby and everything that had happened in the past weeks. I didn't go all the time and distanced myself a little because of the overwhelming feelings I was experiencing.

The paediatrician we had told me we needed to have occupational therapy, physiotherapy and speech therapy for Saxon. So, I was thrust into a world of needing all these resources and therapists, but I was determined to do everything perfectly. I was probably putting too much pressure on myself but that was how I was feeling. I found and engaged private therapists.

There wasn't any subsidised therapy unless you attended them in a group setting. I investigated a group called Biala, but I didn't feel the kids got enough from the therapists. They would come and do five minutes with your child and for me, it wasn't enough. I wanted to do more than that with Saxon.

We engaged private therapists for several years until he started school. We worked on his physical goals of sitting, crawling and walking as well as fine motor skills and a speech therapist. We spent the first four years doing six weekly therapy sessions and activities in between to help him develop.

He enjoyed the therapy. There was a lot of interaction, and it was one to one. A very busy schedule for us but I was determined to do as much for him as I could. When the therapists weren't there, I had exercises I had to do with him so many times a day. I made sure I did everything they said to with him. I felt a lot of pressure to be a good mum and I didn't want him to miss anything. It was a very intense time, but I had a lot of expectations of myself. I thought if I didn't do it all, and perfectly, he might suffer. If I had that time over, I would do things differently even just to take some of that pressure away.

We didn't do any group therapy like Biala because we didn't have a lot of time and their schedule didn't match ours. I was working so the private therapy worked so much better for us at the time.

Saxon is very cheeky, tenacious, very bright and intuitive. He has an extremely strong memory and is full on. Everything is 100 miles an hour 24 hours a day. He's also very social and lots of fun, but never stops. He's on the go all the time and very impulsive.

He has a busy schedule with dance at BAM. He loves his dance classes and all his friends he does that with. Born performer is what he is. He also plays basketball with Special Olympics and loves to go bowling. He regularly bowls every week with a group of friends locally and I love seeing the fun they have and the joy when they are playing.

Going out is another thing he loves to do with seeing a movie, going out for dinner, and even getting takeaway as a treat to have at home is something he looks forward to. He's a very busy boy and as I said earlier, likes to be on the go all the time.

He is not good at stopping and needs to be occupied, stimulated and moving all the time. There's never a time where he would just be sitting on the couch chilling out. I do try and make him sit and relax and we have a routine for this in place but it's only ever in short bursts.

I try to structure it in between his activities and force him to stop and just take a little time to relax. He will do it and play with his toys for a while, but you can see him get restless and that's when he starts asking what is next. What is he going to do next? He will ask over and over again because he just doesn't ever sit. So, he does have downtime, but it's forced by me so he can try learning to just relax sometimes.

He does go to bed early and will often watch a movie before he goes to sleep. But his internal alarm has him up anywhere from 4am. He is quite heavy on his feet and turns on the TV which can wake us all.

He loves people and interacting with them and he's very good with others, always wanting to say hello and chat. I love seeing his face when people interact back with him. He really enjoys that social interaction.

I would love to see everybody, including Saxon, to have the ability to do whatever it is they choose to do and are capable of doing. If there's an activity or a desire for something he wants to do, I would never feel it wasn't possible because he wouldn't be included.

For me it is allowing him to be able to do what he is capable of doing more than anything else because if he wanted to do something, I would make sure he was included. It's important to think like that so we don't put limitations on his inclusion.

I am also very realistic about his capability. For instance, I'm not going to push for him to get his license when I know that's not something he is capable of doing. But, if he wants to go to a dance party or a nightclub or wants to join a program and it's something he is capable of doing, then he should be included regardless. He may need support to do it, but that's okay.

True inclusion isn't unconditional, and I think it must include what that person needs to help them be included. Saxon needs support and I wouldn't expect a group to support his needs on their own. He would need a support person with him to make sure he understands what he needs to understand.

We've never faced any obstacles with any of the programs Saxon is part of and most of what we choose are accommodating of special/additional needs.

In the community, we have come across some interesting people over the years. I remember once a few years ago something that happened in the supermarket. I was trying to teach Saxon how to push the trolley for me while I put the groceries in it. I was trying to get him to have control of it, so he would stop and be safe as we were walking around. It was also something for him to concentrate on rather than just being at the supermarket with me and getting bored.

An old man came up and basically told me, in front of Saxon, that he shouldn't be there. He told me I should have left him at home and done the shopping by myself because he was a nuisance in the supermarket. I was teaching him to be independent and he was not being a nuisance at all. Just because he needed to stop every now and then to gain control of the trolley was not being disruptive to anyone else.

I also had a lady approach me one day when walking in the street with Saxon and question whether he was my son or not. When I told her he was, she proceeded to ask, 'Did you actually give birth to him?' My response was, 'He can hear you, he's standing right here and yes, I did give birth. He is my son.'

The community sometimes surprises me with the things they say, and I've had people challenge me as to whether Saxon is mine. I really don't understand that, because when you look at us, I think we look alike. Not sure what they are seeing.

People have also come up to me and asked me what is wrong with his face. I don't know why they would ask such a thing. His features are fully explainable if you ask me, and he is a gorgeous young man. I see people staring and some will ask that question.

These people, on the whole, are the minority and I find most people are wonderful and accepting. We just live like any other family and do the best we can.

When Saxon was younger it was harder because he would have meltdowns and I wouldn't be able to get him in the pram or out of the pram. Or he would run away and some of his behaviours were very difficult and even now they can be, but I can reason with him most of the time now.

I don't mind people asking me questions because that's how we learn and as I said, most people are wonderful and very kind. The minority, to me, are uneducated and just rude. Questions are fine but think about what you are asking before you open your mouth. Some things people say are very hurtful.

We should all be respectful of other people's feelings. When people ask a rude question, it's very hard, but I always try to use it as an opportunity to educate. But they have to get me on a good day.

People who ask legitimate questions about Saxon always get a great response back from me and it's a much more pleasant experience. Some of the rude questions get responded to the same way depending on what they've asked and how I'm feeling.

I think education and acceptance is key. In the early days, when babies are born, there must be more support when receiving a diagnosis and it needs to be holistic. It needs to be from the hospital to the aftercare, to the environment where they're going to be and there needs to be a facility where the mum and dad can stay with the baby for bonding.

When a baby is born, this is the pathway you should actually take, with proper information around companion cards, supports in the community, access to services, access to other families and it needs to be given at a time when you are ready for it. There definitely needs to be someone holding the family's hand from the very beginning because every situation is different, and everyone has a different home life.

Some mums are working full time, some are single mums and I think that having someone to hold the hand of the family right from the start would benefit the child and the whole family including any siblings. That is what I would like to see more than anything else.

I'd like to see greater awareness because we all fear what we don't understand. Awareness will help to break down the fear and will help the community to open their hearts and be more comfortable.

I'd love people to see life how Saxon sees it. He thinks having Down syndrome and a disability is his superpower and he fully owns it. He will ask me if he has Down syndrome and when I tell him 'Yeah of course you have', he fist pumps the air and says, 'YES!'

I want other people to see that and not only see the beauty in him for feeling like that about himself, but for them to feel like that about themselves. If people feel good about who they are, they'll be kinder to people like Saxon.

That's what I would love. I would love people to have a little bit of him in his self-confidence and self-love. If we could all have that and live a little bit like that, then the world would be a kinder place for everyone.

From the Hearts of Mums

AMY AND TINA
Langwarrin, Melbourne, Australia

Amy, Aged 21 Years

Amy arrived into the world three and a half weeks earlier than expected. After having a few hours of what I thought were Braxton Hicks contractions, my waters broke; I rang the hospital, and the midwife said, 'Sounds like you're having a baby today.'

After getting my mum-in-law out of bed in the wee hours of the morning, and over to our place, we arrived at the hospital around 5am. Amy was born just after midday. I wasn't in labour for that long and all things considered, it was a pretty easy birth.

Amy was handed to me, and I said to my hubby Chris, 'Look she's already got attitude, her tongue is sticking out.' At that time, I didn't realise there was a very good reason why she was doing this.

The nurses were running in and out of the labour room, and fussing all around me, but I didn't see that as being strange, I just thought I was super special. They'd contacted the on-call paediatrician because Amy had arrived early, and it was routine for them to be called for early arrivals, so they were able to check her over. Again, it didn't seem strange because it made perfect sense at the time.

I found out later that they had placed further urgency on the paediatrician coming out to the hospital because they had seen clear signs that Amy had Down syndrome. They were not allowed to tell Chris and I of their perceptions and concerns, as it was something that had to be confirmed by the paediatrician and a subsequent blood test.

The paediatrician that came to see us was Dr Simon Blair who we see till this day. I distinctly remember him arriving in the

Amy, Aged 21 Years

labour room. I was still holding Amy, the midwife was on my left, Chris was on my right. Simon was standing at the end of the bed and started to explain the real reason why he was there.

He told us they suspected Amy had Down syndrome and when he said that to us, for me, it was like having an outer body experience. He started to explain that to confirm this, Amy had to have a blood test, and he didn't like to do any test without having the parents' permission and explaining the reasons for having the test.

He was quite certain Amy did have Down syndrome but the only way they could confirm it was with a blood test. They took her away and I remember Chris and I just looking at each other not really knowing what to say.

We didn't say a lot because we had gone from being on quite a high after having our baby, to quite a low because it was such a shock hearing those words, Down syndrome. It wasn't something we had on our radar or were expecting at all.

We started thinking about all the worst things. We'd heard horror stories and many negative things, so I think our minds were going to that place when we first heard the words Down syndrome.

When Simon came back with Amy, I just kept looking at her because I couldn't see what they were seeing. I stared at her for quite a while wondering what they could see that I couldn't.

It suddenly dawned on me why I'd had so much attention in the labour room as soon as she was born; all the nurses were coming in to look at Amy and then confirming with each other outside of the labour room, what they were seeing. They wanted to be certain I guess before they called the doctor.

She did have many of the markers once they were explained to us. She had the tongue protrusion, a large space between the big toe and the second toe, the almond shaped eyes, the flat nose and compared to my first daughter Jenni, Amy was very floppy (hypotonia, poor muscle tone). One thing she didn't have was the crease across the palm of her hand which is also quite common for people with Down syndrome.

When I look back, it was a great pregnancy but strangely enough, I did have a feeling that something wasn't quite right. I didn't know what to do about the feeling I had, and I didn't really think to tell anyone, not even Chris.

Simon was great and came in to see me six days out of the seven I was in hospital with Amy. I would have lists and lists of questions for him and he would sit in the chair and listen to all my questions so patiently. He was great and answered everything I asked, and I knew we were in great hands with him right from the start.

The nurses in the hospital were also fantastic and very supportive. They let me know Amy was the third baby born at the hospital, with Down syndrome that year, and they put me in touch with Down Syndrome Victoria.

It was very hard telling the rest of the family, but they were all so incredibly supportive. I was so nervous when we told Margaret and Peter, my parents-in-law, but they were great and didn't have anything negative to say at all.

Amy, Aged 21 Years

When I told my brother, the first thing he said was that she could do Special Olympics when she gets older. It's very funny that he said that now because she does do Special Olympics basketball and swimming.

My sister Maureen didn't really say too much, she had quite a lot going on in her life at that time. When I told my other sister Doreen, she told me 'I really didn't need to hear this today, I've had a really bad day.' Yeah, sorry about that. It was after all the fourth anniversary of our mum's passing, not something I planned, but I got a little shitty, ended the call quickly and slammed down the phone. Something you could do back in 2001! I swore loudly, which gained the attention of one of the nurses who came running in to see what all the fuss was about. I explained what my sister had said, and the nurse told me to 'slam away', which made me laugh and lightened the moment.

I had quite varied responses from different friends, most great, one not so. She suggested that Amy had 'a bit of Down syndrome it's not full blown Down syndrome'. Either you have it, or you don't, no such thing as a little bit Down syndrome.

Marie said, 'I hate to ask this, but are they sure?' Which made me laugh.

My friend Kim was amazing. When dropping my eldest daughter at her house to take Amy to her first early intervention group, I told Kim I just didn't want to go, it meant that it was real, and I just couldn't get my head around it. She said that you know you've got to do this, it is what Amy needs and what you need. It'll be hard, but she knew I could do it.

Sally, another friend, when I told her about Amy, 'Oh I bet she's still beautiful' were the first words that came out.

Within the first week of Amy being born, we had been overwhelmed with advice and information, so that we had become experts. Many people were telling us what they knew, and what someone else had told them and so on, and so on. We were overloaded with information and had to just say 'no more!'

I shed a lot of tears when Amy was first born. A lot of self-doubt crept in. I really didn't think I was capable of looking after this baby. With all the years of abuse I had put up with at the hands of my own father, I somehow felt like I was being punished for something I had done wrong.

This is not what I had planned at all; now I had to change my whole mindset. In the blink of an eye, everything changed. Everything!

You think you're on top of this parenting gig, and then suddenly you feel like a fish out of water not knowing what was going to happen and what direction you're headed in. This wasn't what we were expecting and wasn't what was supposed to be happening, so it's very natural to go through negative emotions.

We were also only going to ever have one child. Chris already had two children from his previous marriage, and I managed to convince him that 'just one more' is all I wanted and talked him into it. So, when we were told about Amy having Down syndrome, I felt awful. What have I done? It was all I kept thinking. What have I done?

Amy, Aged 21 Years

Between the birth of our two girls, Chris and I had actually had a conversation, where he'd said he wouldn't know how he'd cope if we had a child with a disability. Yet when it happens, you cope; and cope we did and still do.

Part of coping and managing when you receive a diagnosis like Down syndrome is support. The hospital had information folders from Down Syndrome Victoria because there had been two bubs born with Down syndrome in the January and February before Amy's birth in March. In the folder there was a poem 'Welcome to Holland' by Emily Pearl Kingsley, where she shares what it's like to have a child with Down syndrome by comparing it to planning a trip to Italy but ending up in Holland. That poem always stays with me, and many family's experiences resonate with exactly what she wrote.

I called Down Syndrome Victoria and spoke to Fae, who was very reassuring. I felt extremely supported and actually ended up running a support/coffee group through DSV for other families which was great. I was also listed as a contact for the referral of new families in my area after they had received a diagnosis of Down syndrome.

A friend of my brother-in-law had a daughter Kelsey, and I was able to be put in touch with them as well. We organised a catch up together with another family that DSV had put me in touch with too. One evening we all went out for dinner. The other mum was telling me all these wonderful stories about her child and how great it is and how well she was doing. And I remember thinking to myself that it can't be that great, it all sounded so rosy and unrealistic, so I cornered Kelsey's mum in the bathroom and asked her if it's all that 'rosy' and straightforward. She was more honest and told me it's a lot of hard work and adds a whole new level to raising your child because of regular doctor visits, specialists, regular health checks, blood tests and many other things that you may not have to deal with otherwise.

We started early intervention with Amy mid-April, a few weeks after she was born. It's group therapy and they have a speech therapist, occupational therapist and a physiotherapist working with the children. I started meeting other parents at this group with children who had various different types of disabilities. It gave me an awareness of what other disabilities there were, and I remember thinking at the time, I guess Down syndrome isn't as complicated as many others, though still not without its challenges.

Biala was great with the therapy they provided; it gave me the opportunities to meet other parents going through the same learning curve as myself. There were some great friendships forged at the time that are still going strong today. I felt so happy and very relieved to meet others travelling on the same journey as me and we were able to share stories and support each other along the way.

The therapy at Biala was with other families and everything was conducted in a group setting. As well as the therapists, there was also a maternal health nurse. We would sit in a circle on the floor and sing songs as well as do massage on the children and other exercises to assist with their muscle tone. Water therapy, combined with our time at Biala, helped Amy enormously with strengthening her muscles.

I found the communication programs the speech therapists used interesting. They used Makaton which is derived from Auslan (Australian Sign Language). They used it in conjunction with speech and signs were used through keywords of a sentence. They used picture exchange (PECS) to help the kids with communication too. A combination of both proved very useful in the early stages of Amy trying to communicate.

One of the things I learned at Biala, were the kids learnt very quickly what they liked to do, and what they didn't. Their favourite sign seemed to be 'finished' which is having the thumb up and shaking the hand back and forth. I think they learned that one fast because they were always happy to be finished and really didn't like the 'exercise' part of the program.

Amy has a sassy and engaging personality; she's cheeky, though she'll tell you she's not, and has a great sense of humour. She's caring and intuitive and for someone who has trouble communicating she is able to pick up when someone is not feeling okay, give them a hug and take away their problem albeit momentarily, but for some reason it gives the receiver of that hug a sense of comfort, and an opportunity to forget about their problem for a while. For Amy it's like her super power, and it's a wonderful attribute to have.

I love how when we're stopped in traffic or at traffic lights, Amy will strike up a conversation with the car next to us. Often, she gets a response, sometimes not; I generally explain that they didn't hear her and she's okay with that. The following conversation took place not so long ago.

'What are you doing?' (All one word).
'Me and my mate are going to the gym, what are you doing?'
Light turns green, drive a short distance then we stop at the next red light. Conversation continues.
'What are you doing?'

'What are you doing?' he asks.
Amy responds, I interpret what she says and tell the lads we're off to catch up with her big sister.
Light turns green, another short distance to the next red light, and the conversation continues.
He asks, 'What's your name?' Interpreter (me) says her name is Amy.
'Hi Amy' he says, 'My name is Rory, hope you have a great time catching up with your sister.'

Rory and his mate head off to the gym as Amy waves to them and they wave back. Amy and I catch up with Jenni at her work. Great afternoon all round. Can't thank Rory enough for his interaction with Amy that day, it was incredible. He made her day, and mine too.

Amy still loves the Wiggles (the original foursome) and watches them constantly much to our despair. You think that after a few years the Wiggles would be replaced, with something, anything! But no. I've been hearing (not listening) to the Wiggles since Jenni was born in 1997 to this very day. I can credit them with getting Amy up and about and moving, but when you find yourself singing Wiggles songs when they're not even being played, you know there's a problem.

Inclusion for Amy has always been a bit hit and miss. It takes a while to find your place and it did take a while for us and Amy to find where she fits in, where she feels comfortable and where she can be herself without the judgement of others. If you think Amy doesn't understand what's going on around her, think again. Amy knows when she is not being accepted, and knows when she is not comfortable and that she doesn't fit in.

Amy, Aged 21 Years

We tried dual schooling in the first two years of her education. One day a week at mainstream primary school and the other four at Special Development School. The one day a week was always a Monday, and the other students in Amy's prep class were very welcoming of her, as was her teacher. Her aide, Julie was amazing, and everything seemed to move along quite nicely, and Amy slowly started up a couple of little friendships, and got the odd party invitation here and there.

As much as everyone was accepting of the one day at school, Amy herself wasn't entirely happy. About eighteen months in, halfway through year one, her behaviour started to change, she became disruptive in the classroom, and started to spend less time in the classroom setting and more time outside. Inclusion wasn't happening, not because of the school, other kids, the teacher or the setting as such. Amy just wasn't comfortable, and she made that apparent by her behaviour. The decision to go full time to the Special Development School was made, and we never looked back. She was in a place where she was comfortable, happy, safe and most of all accepted for who she was.

Another place she feels most at home is her swimming. We tried the mainstream swimming programs, where eventually she would just stand in the shallow end of the pool and refuse to do anything. The swimming teachers were given permission to make her do things, but they said they were not allowed to push the students, the students had to make their own decisions as to what they wanted to do. So, after about six to eight months of sheer frustration, spending a considerable amount of money and getting nowhere I withdrew her from the classes and enrolled Amy into swimming classes with our local Special Olympics program.

All I wanted was for Amy to be safe around water and be able get herself to safety should she ever fall in the water. Six months into this program, the swimming coach had her doing just that and more. The other swimmers in the program were all at various levels of ability, and Amy still attends this program and has made some very good friends along the way.

Since finishing school, Amy attends a day program for adults with disabilities. There are a number of establishments in our area who offer programs to adults with special needs. And like a needle in a haystack, you have to find the one that you think will 'fit' your young adult. Fortunately, in Amy's last year of school, one of her teachers took a number of parents to have a look at the local programs. To give us a feel for them. It was a great thing to do and certainly helped me in working out the best placement for Amy.

The day program Amy attends is a perfect 'fit' for her. When she started, there were already some past students and school friends attending the centre. Right away she was comfortable, and within a very short time made her presence felt. They absolutely love her there, they love her sassiness, her cheekiness and of course her cuddles. She is greeted everyday by her peers, and the support workers with such adoration and it is heart-warming to know that she has found her place. She is included, feels included and knows that she is safe.

We've had many an obstacle in the years since Amy was born, and it has come in various different settings and formats – from the reactions of everyday people you meet to communication on medical issues and dealings with government bodies. It varies so much, it's really hard to pinpoint.

Amy, Aged 21 Years

We all know Down syndrome is a permanent disability, however when it comes to Australian Federal Government run bodies such as Medicare and Centrelink it doesn't seem to register to them that it is permanent. After filling in the appropriate paperwork, our family received carer's allowance, a sum of money to assist in helping with the medical side of Down syndrome where you are constantly in and out of specialist appointments to help keep your child well. When Amy turned four, I received a letter from Centrelink asking if her condition had changed. Unfortunately, I ignored it; because of course it's a permanent disability we're talking about here. Four weeks later, her concession card and the Carer's allowance was cancelled.

Upon calling Centrelink to have everything reinstated I am asked that stupid question once more. My response, 'Unless you're aware of a cure for Down syndrome that I'm not, then no, her condition is pretty much the same as it was the day she was born.' Telling me my response was not fair, made me all the more frustrated. The allowance and concession card were reinstated, only to have to go through the whole process again, when she reached secondary school age and then again at the age of sixteen. As a parent, it is an incredibly frustrating and demeaning thing to have to reiterate at stages through our child's life, that they have a permanent disability when it's so blindingly obvious.

Communication is an incredible obstacle for us and Amy. I have to speak on her behalf when we are visiting doctors and specialists, and sometimes they'll ask a question that not even I can answer. Amy has a very high tolerance for pain, which can be good but some of the time it can be very dangerous. In one instance, it was life threatening. At nine months of age, Amy developed a fever, we'd had three nights of no sleep, Amy refusing to feed, and not sleeping herself, high temperatures and vomiting up bright yellow fluid.

A telephone conversation with her paediatrician was to tell me to head straight to emergency and he will call ahead to let them know I was coming in with Amy. Pneumonia was her paediatricians main concern. After being examined, the emergency doctor suggested that they wouldn't bother with an X-ray because they couldn't hear a rattle, so they were quite certain it wasn't pneumonia.

My mum-in-law was with me and suggested quite firmly that they should X-ray her, even if only to eliminate the diagnosis of pneumonia. Reluctantly, they carried out the X-ray, and when the result was confirmed, they could not look me in the eye. Amy was hospitalised for three nights with pneumonia. Prior to that X-ray they were in the process of sending me home with one very sick baby.

Expectation is another obstacle; people see the disability and expect Amy not to be able to do certain things without giving her a chance to have a go and therefore exclude her. There are many things Amy can do, and it's basically whether she wants to do them or not and this is a choice only she makes.

The community as a whole, is slowly making changes to itself to be more inclusive. That has come with a whole lot of effort from those within the 'disability' community and has been years in the making. There is still quite a long way to go, but we are slowly getting the message out there that our young people can be very productive members of the community. They have the same needs and wants as everyone else, we just have to take the time to listen and learn.

Amy, Aged 21 Years

Amy has been a great teacher, not only to us, but to all those who know her. She has taught us:

- To be resilient, to stand up for what is right, and don't take any crap from anyone. That saying 'no' is okay. You can't do everything.

- Patience – she has tested ours to within an inch of itself, so much so, I've often said that 'Patience' is my middle name.

- To live your best life, and don't give a crap what someone else thinks about you.

- To fight for what is fair. Throughout every major hurdle we've had to overcome we've had to put on our boxing gloves and go for it. Not all the doctors and specialists know what's right for her, and we can question them when we know that they're being dismissive of our concerns.

- To 'dance like nobody's watching'. To let go of the life we were expecting to live and live in the 'now'. Look at life through her eyes. And, that the Wiggles will remain a permanent fixture in our lives for ever and ever.

She can be herself, and people will love her for who she is, not what she was born with.

If we all lived in Amy's world, it'd be a much happier place to live.

From the Hearts of Mums

JOEL AND ISOBEL
Somerville, Melbourne, Victoria

Joel, Aged 22 Years

Joel was born at 39 weeks, and we didn't know he had Down syndrome before he was born. We weren't expecting to hear news of that nature at all.

It was very quick as we were told immediately after he arrived that they thought he may have Down syndrome. It felt like five minutes after he was born that they were telling us there were signs and common markers.

James, my husband, had Joel in his arms when they told us but just about collapsed on the floor. All I cared about was seeing my little boy and wanted to hold him. I was also exhausted and wasn't really taking anything they were saying in but kept telling them to give me my baby.

A doctor and paediatrician came into me that morning to tell me they were going to send his blood tests off so they could give a definitive diagnosis. They never really said anything for certain as they needed to wait for results, but we were pretty sure just because of what they had been saying.

All I wanted was my baby in my arms and to get some rest because all the talk was very frightening to me. It was a shock and something we definitely were not expecting.

I wasn't worried about the diagnosis of Down syndrome, but it was still a shock hearing those words. I had previously worked in a respite house, and we had residents there with Down syndrome, so I knew some information about it.

When we took Joel home it became very scary. I'm a qualified childcare worker and had worked in disability so if anyone could do this, it was me, but I wasn't coping. James was freaking out as well which I don't think helped how I was feeling, but it was a scary time for both of us. I really was feeling like a useless mother and a useless childcare worker at the time.

He was our first child and our miracle child. We were told I wouldn't be able to have children because I'd had an ectopic rupture years before. When I was having my surgery at the time, the doctor told me the other tube was stuck to the wall. He said it was unlikely I would ever have children.

So, when I became pregnant with Joel, we were overjoyed and couldn't believe it. I really enjoyed being pregnant, and it was such a joy watching my belly grow and knowing there was a little person in there that would make us a family.

When you hear the news that you are going to be travelling down a very different path than you had envisaged, it takes a while to process everything but if you have good support, you can get through those times.

We had specialists like physio, speech and occupational therapy come to our house when we first brought Joel home. They would come in and do exercises with him and give me things to do with him when they weren't there.

They said they loved coming to work with us because they knew I would do the exercises they gave me to do when they weren't there. For me, being a childcare worker, if someone teaches you something and gives it to you to do, you do it.

We would do the exercises regularly and as he got a little older, he was beginning to learn how to walk up steps. This was a dilemma in my head because we didn't have any steps at all in our house. I didn't know how I was going to continue teaching him this and then they said, what about the curb outside? It never occurred to me. So, we went outside and practised on the curb. It worked so well.

It was great having such supportive people around us because the doctors were not very positive at all about Joel having Down syndrome. I found them to be very clinical. But one thing we didn't get, because we had a postnatal diagnosis, were the details about termination.

I remember we were handed a booklet about Down syndrome and the first chapter was filled with all the negative things about it. I couldn't get past the first two pages, it terrified me.

Once we got home, we had to find a GP for Joel and I looked everywhere for a doctor that would see Joel as a person before the Down syndrome. I wanted someone that wouldn't blame Down syndrome for everything that was going on with him like chicken pox because we all know it has nothing to do with that.

We did find a wonderful GP who treated Joel with so much respect. He talks to him and interacts with him in such a caring way. He's a lot further away than I would have liked, but it's so worth it. He is very supportive of us all as a family and I'm so pleased I found him.

It was so hard finding someone like him. Someone that didn't blame Down syndrome for all the ailments he had. There are some things that are Down syndrome specific, but there are a lot that aren't. I wasn't an expert back then like I am now so it was very important to find a supportive doctor that would treat us with respect and listen.

Joel, Aged 22 Years

Even the nurses at the hospital I found to be unsupportive. We had this wonderful midwife while we were going to the prenatal classes, but when Joel was born, she didn't come near me. Didn't even come to see if I was alright. It was as though she was frightened to come in and see me and my baby. It made me feel like having Joel wasn't wonderful to her and I didn't really understand it. She was a midwife and I'm sure she had come across babies with Down syndrome before.

According to them while I was in there, it was a tragedy. What?!! No, it's not a tragedy at all. I had a baby, and I needed some help, and they weren't helping me.

When I was doing my studies, I taught women how to breastfeed and now I needed help. It was so different being on the other side. I had so much milk, I could have fed the whole nursery, but my Joel wouldn't drink. It was a nightmare, spurting everywhere and when I was trying to get help, there was nobody.

It made me feel so isolated and I know there were lots of babies in the special care nursery they were looking after, but I had a little boy with Down syndrome that wouldn't drink, and I needed help. I had no support at all in the hospital from any of the medical staff and I hoped when we went home our family and friends would be different.

Family reaction was interesting, and I have many stories about that time. When I was pregnant, we knew we were having a boy and we named him Joel and shared that with everyone. When my mother-in-law came into the hospital, I was in the breastfeeding room trying to coordinate all of that.

A nurse came in and said they had someone at the reception desk, and she thought it was my mother-in-law. She said she thought James should go and speak with her. Very strange if you ask me, so I asked what was going on. She told me that she came in and told her she wanted to see the Down syndrome baby. Now, you must remember, this was her grandson she was speaking about.

I couldn't believe my ears. I told the nurse she had known for months that we were having a boy and she knew his name. She didn't even tell the nurse our surname because she had an issue about that as well. We joined our surnames together with a hyphen when we got married and she didn't approve.

When James went to speak with her, she told him it must be from my side because we don't have anything like that on our side. I was furious with her and never forgave her. She passed away a couple of years after Joel was born, and let's just say we weren't friends when she passed.

My brother was another one who astounded me by his reaction. He never really said a lot until Joel was two and he and his partner were having a baby. His wife had gone for an ultrasound and when he came to see me, he asked why I didn't have an ultrasound or any tests. I told him I did, and nothing was picked up, but I wouldn't have done anything anyway.

His response to that was that he didn't want anything like that in his family. I told him well, Joel is your family and then I told him very loudly to get the hell out of my house. I haven't spoken to him since that day. I can't believe our family responded like that, but they have now missed out on an incredible boy that would have loved them unconditionally.

Joel, Aged 22 Years

A lot of my friends said they were sorry, but nobody means anything negative with that, because it's a response that people say when they don't know what to say. They just don't know how else to respond.

One friend, who was a pro at breastfeeding, started looking things up when I told her I was having trouble feeding Joel. After she had finished looking up 'breastfeeding a Down syndrome baby', her response to me was 'well, other people can do it'. No tips or strategies that may help, nothing from her at all except for that.

I also told that friend how I was feeling and that not one person had even sent any flowers congratulating us on the birth of our son. She must have got straight on the phone and started calling everyone, because over the next couple of days, I was receiving flowers at a rapid rate. I had so many. Pity I had to basically ask for them to receive them.

There was some positivity, and it came from a 15-year-old boy where we went to church. His parents were the pastors, and they came in to see me. They were terrific and he wanted to come in and see me. He told them he didn't care if Joel had Down syndrome, he wanted to meet him. He said, 'I've been waiting for him for months, and now I want to see him'.

It really warmed my heart and made me happy that he wanted to see him. When he came in, he was just in awe of our little boy and the love he felt shone brightly. This was something that really lifted my spirits and something I needed. This boy is a man and a father himself now, and I know, because of the way he was with Joel, that he is an amazing father.

It was difficult having the negativity around me with everyone and even support back then was a little difficult to find. I called Down Syndrome Victoria, but they didn't have anyone at that stage that I could connect with. They did have people that helped come and support families, but at the time, that support had dried up.

When Joel was about two years old, I found out about a lady in Langwarrin that wanted to start running a coffee/support group. I can't even remember how I found out about her, but it could have been the local paper.

I was nervous, but I desperately needed some support, so I decided to join her group. Of course, my mind started wandering and I was thinking about the fact I didn't know her and what if she wasn't nice. First step was a phone call, and she was amazing and so lovely. I couldn't wait to meet her after that call.

I went to my first coffee group, and it was exactly what I needed. These women were a breath of fresh air and such great support. It was every fortnight, and I was always there before the start time and was the last to leave. It really was wonderful.

When Joel was born it was pre-internet days, so searching things up like services and support was not as easy as it is now. So, groups like Tina's were like finding gold. It was great connecting with other mums with kids with Down syndrome and providing support for each other. Sharing many things like therapies, what we were doing with our kids at home, and it was great for the kids to make friends.

Now, there are lots of online support groups people can join to ask questions and even talk to other families. We all learned about online support when Covid hit, and we were all locked down. There definitely seems to be a lot more available for new families now which is great.

Taking that first step with Tina was hard. I didn't know her or how old her child was. I didn't know how old she was or how many other people would be there. I wondered what she would be able to help me with and had all kinds of thoughts going through my head.

Little did I know that I would get a lot of help from the people at this group who had children that were older than Joel. I didn't have a phobia of meeting people, but I was nervous about going to this group for the first time. After a couple of times with these ladies, it was like the whole world had opened for me. I knew these were my people and they were the ones that would understand everything I was going through.

It's so important to be around like-minded people. Just like when you have your first child (without a disability), and you get put in a 'first mums' group with others entering the world of motherhood for the first time.

You sit there and you're all going through the same thing. Whereas at home you feel like you're the only one going through these things. You feel like your child is the only one doing certain things and it's not until you meet other mums that you see their children are going through the same things. It's also great because you can bounce ideas off each other and most importantly, give the support that is so needed.

I was in a pre-natal class, and we did try to form a group with those families, but it didn't work. The hospital we were at was the South Eastern Hospital and the families came from many different areas. It just didn't work.

I also tried joining the local first mums' group, but all the kids were doing so many things that Joel wasn't and for me, it was depressing. Then I found Tina and I knew this was the group for me. To have these people who knew exactly what it was like, some having younger kids and some having older. They knew exactly what I was talking about all the time, and I really loved that.

Joel was a wonderful baby which I'm so grateful for because that made things easier. He giggled a lot, and we have recordings of him doing this and we still listen to them every now and then when we are feeling a little down. It kills me, I love it. Always puts a smile on my face and makes me laugh.

He was always very engaging, and he loved being out and about. People would come over to look at him because he was a baby, but when they looked at him, they would say 'oh'. I would try to keep the smile on my face, but it was very hard. Especially because he was so engaging and really loved seeing people.

I loved dressing him up, but he was born in November and that year was the hottest November we had for a long time. Most of the time he was in singlet and nappy, so I had all these beautiful outfits that he never got to wear. Everything was tie dyed so at least he was colourful.

We did a lot of exercises and other things with him on the floor to help him reach his milestones. We were seeing a physio, an OT and a speech therapist and I learned so much from them. We would see the speech therapist once every two months and the others we would see monthly. What they showed me to do with Joel, helped with my job as a childcare worker because there were lots of blowing cotton balls across the table and other activities like that.

We experimented with soft foods and allowed him to play with it for the texture. The speech therapist said it would be good for him to do this. We've got photos of him with the dog and spaghetti everywhere, all over his face.

He was a funny little man because when he was born, he didn't fit into his skin. He was like the saggy baggy elephant, so I was always on the floor doing things with him and trying different foods to build everything up. Within three months he started chunking up and he hasn't stopped ever since. I am concerned about it now and I do try and monitor what he is eating, but it's very difficult.

I remember also spending a lot of time with Joel at Southland Shopping Centre because it was so hot, and we didn't have cooling in the house. I knew where everything was, the toilets on every floor, the change areas, the family rooms. I did a lot of things on my own with Joel back then and I did start to fall into a depression.

One time I went to see my sister in Warragul because I really needed some help. I told her I wasn't coping well. I thought she would be helpful, but she wasn't. She just kept telling me he's okay and he's fine.

On the drive home that day, I remember wondering if I could guarantee that Joel and I would die if I hit a tree while travelling at 100kph. I couldn't guarantee that in my head, so I just kept driving home. I told James I was sick when we got home, and I needed some serious help.

It scared the hell out of me, but it was a turning point where I began to get the help I needed and start pulling myself together. That all happened before I met Tina and the wonderful group she was running. I guess we need to hit a breaking point before we can start to heal sometimes, and things did start falling into place after that moment.

Today, Joel is 22 and things are a lot different now. He makes me laugh daily and he has a very quick wit. He runs his own business making dog biscuits called Joel's Canine Cookie Co. I am so very proud of him.

He has support workers that help him make the biscuits and we help him from time to time. But he knows all the steps and every single ingredient that goes into them. He says it very proudly – oats, peanut butter and pumpkin – and he will always tell you exactly what's in them.

The other thing he does with his business that he loves and is very good at, is merchandise. He loves merchandise and has t-shirts, bags and coffee cups and is always coming up with new ideas. I didn't even know what it was when he first mentioned it. He has come up with the idea of mini treats for dogs now because he said there are little dogs that find it hard to eat the bigger cookies, so they need small ones so it's easier.

He has theories about everything and even has a theory for The Big Bang Theory. At night he sits in his room writing on pieces of paper about all the theories he has, certain characters and the way they behave and what they do. He loves making up theories about Shark Boy and Lava Girl – I didn't even know who they were.

Joel, Aged 22 Years

He loves to write, and the funny thing about that is that I didn't even know he could write. I knew he recognised letters and certain words but I never realised he could write the way he does.

What he does is get on the internet and asks Google how to spell certain words. If he says the word clearly enough, Google will tell him. Because his language is not always clear, Google has led him up some funny paths.

I can hear him at night yelling at Google with the words he wants to use, and sometimes getting frustrated. But he continues to try so he can get the result he wants. We have paper everywhere and all over his bedroom, but it's something he likes to do and while he's doing it, he's learning.

He loves basketball and plays once a week but other exercise, forget it! I'm grateful he loves basketball because at least he is getting some sort of exercise. Very difficult to get him to go on a walk and I don't think he would even enter a gym.

He loves the internet and yells at us when we turn it off. We turn it off at 10pm every night to stop him from staying up all night with it. He's learned though, and downloads things to his iPad or tablet so he can do things once it's off. Very clever.

He loves to sing and often watches his favourite songs on his devices and sings at the top of his voice. He makes up his own rap songs mostly about how mean his dad is. He says dad turns off the internet, so he's mean. Tells me he loves me, which I love but when I betray him by turning off the internet, I'm also the mean one.

He talks to himself very often which I enjoy listening to because this is the only time, he speaks about exactly how he is feeling. Everything that is going on in his head, he tells himself. He won't always open up and tell us, so when he talks to himself, I listen because then I know what is going on and how he is feeling.

He is a night owl and often stays awake in his room until 6am. We know because when his dad gets up to go to work, he yells out, 'Goodnight, I'm going to bed now.' I try and get him to go to bed and often get up and down during the night, but he does have an answer for me. He tells me he's an adult and can do whatever he likes. Tells me I can't tell him what to do.

I do tell him it's not for me, it's for him. I try and explain that if he goes to sleep earlier, he can get up early and do the things he wants to do. He does have activities he has to do during the day, but he still insists on staying up until the crack of dawn.

He is such a character and there are so many things I could share about Joel. I could write a book just on the funny things he says and does. He loves to laugh and make us laugh.

Joel and his sister Mietta have a typical sibling relationship with arguments and saying they don't like each other, but they do have lots of lovely moments together. I do worry about Mietta because she wants to get her licence but feels guilty because Joel won't get his. She doesn't want to upset him. I tell her she can take him for drives just the two of them and make some lovely memories together.

It's the same with having a boyfriend. She doesn't want to hurt him because she knows he would love to have a girlfriend. He desperately wants to have a girlfriend he can go out with and have fun with.

They are typical siblings, and their relationship can be quite difficult at times. I shake my head, but I know they love each other because they show me, and each other, that all the time. Mietta does always want to include him in things and she does worry about his feelings when it comes to things she knows he may never be able to do.

There are many things Joel can do, and he does them well. I would love for people not to be surprised at what he can do. When we are out sometimes people speak to me and ask me what he would like when they should be asking him.

Our local community is great as everyone has gotten to know Joel and they do say hello to him, and Joel loves to talk to them all. Very social boy he is. Most of the time people are great and say hello to him when he says hello to them. He loves that because he feels part of the community.

There was one time in the supermarket when a lady was standing behind him. He kept saying hello to her and she kept ignoring him and looking elsewhere. He said hello to her for the sixth time, and I had enough by this stage. I told him that sometimes people don't want to talk to you mate and that's a bit sad for them because they miss out on getting to know you. He told me, yes like you mum because you love me.

It's not hard just to be kind and say hello back to someone. This was many years ago and as I said, in our local community everyone knows and speaks to him, and I have also become Joel's mum. I don't really mind, but occasionally I'd like to be Isobel. Ha-ha.

He manages his own dog biscuit business and does extremely well and I'd love for people not to be surprised by this. He has been taught the skills and has learned everything he needs to for his business. He's always thinking of new things and new merchandise that he can offer to his customers.

I'm not surprised at the business, but I am surprised at how far he's come with it and how much he has learned. I don't know why I'm surprised and maybe it's not really that; maybe it's just pride that I feel.

People ask me why we didn't investigate a sheltered workshop, Coles, or another job like that, but Joel made the decision to start his own business and we supported him in that choice. He does what he loves to do, and he is extremely good at it. You give anyone the tools and education in what they want to do, and they will do well.

I have friends with children with complex disabilities, but all these children still have a voice and still need to be heard. They have likes and dislikes as we all do, and they know what they want to do and achieve. We need to listen to them and give them the tools and guidance to accomplish these things.

Joel has even learned about business expenses compared to living expenses and other things like that. He has a business card and uses it for the business only. He collects all his receipts and stores them in a file. Even when I do some shopping for the business, he always questions me and wants to see what I've bought to make sure it's only for the business.

He has people that assist him, and they love all his ideas. They tell me he has so many, and they help him to develop these ideas.

Joel, Aged 22 Years

Sometimes it may take a while, but he learns and tries his best. It's great to watch.

I think this is why he doesn't sleep at night. His brain is on overdrive because of all the thinking he is doing and all the ideas he is coming up with. The lady he has helping him is amazing and embraces everything he comes up with. She sees him and hears him and sometimes I think she does that even more than I do. Maybe it's because I don't think of ways to help him to make his ideas come to life, but she has the strategies.

I would love everyone to be more like her and see and hear people. Give them the tools and assistance to learn and grow. Whether there is a disability or not, it's important to see a person's potential and if you are able to facilitate helping them, then do it. Even if all it is, is saying hello back to someone when they say hello to you.

Recently James and I were out, and we saw a young man in a wheelchair with two support workers. They were talking amongst themselves and ignoring him, so he started saying hello to everyone walking by. People were ignoring him, so we went over, and I said hello back to him.

He was so happy. He just wanted someone to talk to and interact with him. I felt so happy that I was able to put a smile on his face and I was so cross at his workers. I wish I knew who his family were so I could tell them what they were doing. It's just not right.

I would also like people to understand that just because two people have Down syndrome, or any other disability, doesn't mean they're the same. We are all different, and I mean all of us. With or without a disability.

People with Down syndrome have something to give and say, and for the record, they are not always happy. They have opinions and they get sad and upset just like we all do. Joel definitely has opinions on many different things.

He doesn't care who is around and still always hugs me and gives me a kiss no matter where we are. I often get comments from others saying they wish their kids still did that. Joel does that because he doesn't worry about what people think. And if he saw someone else doing that to their mum, he wouldn't judge them.

One of the things I really love about Joel is the non-judgement. He takes everyone for who they are no matter what and if you are kind to him, he will be kind back to you and he will like you. All his emotions are unconditional and true.

He is very forgiving and forgives quickly unless you're his father and turn off the internet. That he doesn't forgive so quickly for. He also gets cross and gets upset with me because I don't wear shoes. He tells me I need to wear shoes when I go out, but I never have so I tell him don't have to. I laugh because usually it's the other way around.

He makes me happy and laugh all the time. He recently wanted to get some colourful streaks in his hair and told me it was like me. I asked him if he would go purple hair like me and he told me 'I don't want to be that much like you'.

He's an amazing boy and I love him to bits.

Follow Joel's Canine Cookie Co here - https://www.facebook.com/search/top?q=joels%20canine%20cookie%20co

Joel, Aged 22 Years

NINO AND SHARON
Bristol, United Kingdom

Nino, Aged 24 Years

Nino was born in 1998 and when he arrived, everything was fine. There was never any mention of Down syndrome at the birth or indeed afterwards once home.

He developed extreme reflux and constipation and began failing to thrive. He wasn't gaining weight because he was constantly sick, so our GP monitored him for a while. This went on until he was just over four months old, then they sent us to hospital for him to be monitored overnight.

They wanted to check his feeding and try to work out what was causing the reflux and constipation. He was bottle-fed which may have been what was causing the problems, but breastfeeding wasn't working well for him, so we really had no choice.

We received what felt like a miracle cure of Gaviscon and after four days we were sent home and told to come back in two weeks for a clinic review. There was still no mention of Down syndrome at this stage, and we definitely didn't have it on our radar.

When we arrived at the review, we sat down to wait, then my ex-husband went to the bathroom. When the consultant came out, he asked if I was ready with Nino but when he saw his dad wasn't with us, he asked where he was and said we would wait so he could also come into the room.

That was a red flag immediately for me because I wondered why we needed his dad in the room before I could go in if we were only having a follow-up visit? Nino was almost six months old at this stage and apart from the reflux and constipation, he was doing great, and we had no questions about anything else.

Nino, Aged 24 Years

When we went into the room, there was a nurse sitting at the back of the room. I thought this was strange, because there was never normally anyone else in the consultant's room unless he had a student working with him or something like that.

The atmosphere in the room, and her sitting there with her head down, was very strange but we discovered why they were behaving like this when he began to speak.

He said, 'I'm really sorry to tell you, Nino will never get a normal job – he has Down syndrome'. He carried on talking about all that Nino wouldn't achieve or be able to do and then began a physical check of Nino on the bed. I had completely tuned out at this point and the silence I heard was deafening as I tried to understand what he had just said, 'never get a normal job'.

He then went on to tell us that they took bloods while we were in hospital. I didn't even know they did that. Nobody told us. Apparently when the doctors were doing their rounds while we were in hospital, they noticed his almond shaped eyes and that his head was slightly flat on one side. They told the consultant, and he told them to do the blood tests, but they didn't ever tell us or why. It just all seemed routine, and I never questioned anything they did then.

They didn't tell us. They didn't ask us if it was okay. If I knew then what I know now, I would have said something to him that day, but I didn't. First-time mum and quite shocked at what we had just heard.

He told us the blood tests confirmed that Nino had Trisomy 21 (Down syndrome). He said Trisomy 21, which is the most common type of Down syndrome, and then proceeded to say it was likely he has Mosaic Down syndrome which is another type of Down syndrome.

He told us the geneticist would explain and tell us more and they had made an appointment for us to see them. We went from having a check-up from a hospital stay, to being told our son had Down syndrome and we had to go and see a geneticist.

We were living near Bath at the time and my ex-husband's family were close to the hospital so we went straight there after our appointment. My family were living in Manchester so were too far for us to visit at that time and they had already been to see us the day Nino was born.

We visited his family after the appointment full of shock and a few tears from receiving the news. Nino was six months old, so it was a complete shock for us. His family are Italian/Irish and for them it didn't matter. They told us God had given us a gift and we didn't even need to think twice about it.

Apart from that, it's never really been spoken about in depth again. Nino is Nino and he is our child. It was as simple as that. They were supportive right from the start and always have been which has been wonderful.

My family were the same. They told us we were blessed with our beautiful boy and have always treated him like any other child. They've always accepted him for who he is. None of our family and friends have ever been any different. They've always been amazingly supportive.

My dad had passed away, but we always tell Nino he would have loved him, and he would have. We are from a Catholic

Nino, Aged 24 Years

background, and we have disability in the family with my cousin. Disability was never an issue in our big Irish family because everyone was always accepted.

Nino's dad's family never really spoke about Down syndrome, but my family did and that was fine. I never minded speaking about it because it is a big part of Nino. I also enjoyed the fact that his dad's family never really spoke about it. I loved that it was not a big deal for them, and he was accepted as Nino from the moment he was born and after we received the diagnosis.

We were lucky to be surrounded by loving family members who grew to love Nino regardless of anything else.

I was in complete denial for years and rejected support at home because I just never believed the diagnosis. I always thought they had mixed up the blood tests – I was sure of it. But looking back now, it was just my way of dealing with it all I suppose. I always just treated him as my son and went about bringing him up as best I could, devoting my every moment to making his life the best it could be.

He attended a mainstream nursery and school and had a support assistant in primary school who was amazing and out of this world with the care and support given to Nino. However, it became apparent that this placement wasn't going to continue working because the gap in the age was getting quite big at around seven years old. The girls babied him because he was so cute, and the boys liked to get him into trouble by making him do things he shouldn't.

It was at this time, when we were transitioning to specialist education that I began to face the fact that Nino had Down syndrome. I'd always accepted him for who he was, but I never embraced his diagnosis, so the grieving and emotions really started for me then when he was seven. It wasn't as though I didn't know Nino had Down syndrome, but I always just pushed it to the side and got on with things without thinking about it.

We were lucky because we also always had great support from family and friends. The consultant who spoke with us also sent a letter with everything mentioned and I still have it and reflect on it now after many years have passed.

His words, 'Nino will never get a normal job because he has Down syndrome' have always stayed with me.

I think the language from doctors and consultants needs a lot of improvement. They need to give you the diagnosis and talk to you about what it could mean, but they also need to speak about the positive side of everything.

They do not predict a neurotypical baby's future in its first months of life, so what right do they have to do it for a baby born with an additional chromosome? Especially emphasising the negatives and ignoring the positives!

I remember the geneticist wanted to do more testing on him at the time and I refused it. I didn't see the point really, we had the diagnosis and I just wanted to get home and get on with things.

We had his heart checked and it was fine, and from that moment we didn't really have anything to do with the consultant or geneticist. We saw our GP who was amazing and very supportive with any issues we had.

Nino, Aged 24 Years

They have always been there for us and still are to do this day. Very supportive and very positive with everything that Nino needs.

The only other people we had assist Nino were his therapists. He had input from age three with a speech and language therapist. This is when we both started learning Makaton as well to support his language development and as a communication aid for him.

The therapy began in Nino's early years and the speech and language therapy was ongoing until he left education in 2020. During his specialist school days, the therapy was group therapy with the other children in his class.

He had the one-to-one therapy when he was quite young and then the group therapy in school. It worked well for him and his peers. He has always had speech and language assistance, but the physical therapy and OT finished quite some time ago.

Nino changed schools a couple of times because when he was at a mild learning difficulty school, he got bullied by one of his so-called friends. It was because of this, that he changed his school to Warmley Park School and College in Bristol. He was 14 when this happened, and changing schools was the best thing he could have done.

It was his favourite place to be, and he really thrived when he began attending there. It is the school I work at and when he was younger, he was offered a place there which we declined. I never should have done that, but we had heard of a boy who had difficult behaviours, so we chose the other school.

However, that boy ended up moving to our school a few years later and was in the same class as Nino. This was the boy that was bullying him, and it wasn't long after that, we moved schools. As I said earlier, it was the best decision and Nino loved his new school. He still remembers it as one of his favourite places ever.

The friends he made at that school are the friends he still has to this day. They do so many things together and I'm so pleased he has such a wonderful friendship group. I never have to worry when they are out together because they all really look out for one another. They have a wonderful bond.

He also did a full circle from attending the school to returning last year to coach Rugby in the College, a real success story. Warmley Park is the most amazing specialist setting and I will always be grateful for the education, care, support, fun and love he received from all the staff there over the years he attended.

When Nino was a baby, he was phenomenal. He was cute, gorgeous, and adorable and such a great baby even with the issues we had with him at the start. I really wish I could do it all over again like Groundhog Day – over and over with him and his sister Lia.

Medically, in the early years, it was tough because he had a low immunity as well as the reflux and constipation. We spent a lot of time in hospital and in winter he was always getting chest infections, conjunctivitis and other things like that.

We received a diagnosis from the doctor and then ended up going to a specialist. She was a locum with our GP and from Spain. She took Nino under her wing and began doing lots of tests. She developed a combination of medication to support his asthma, low immunity, allergies and hay fever.

Nino, Aged 24 Years

He's never had conjunctivitis again and rarely has had chest infections. He was also diagnosed with asthma and has inhalers for that. She was amazing. She was a brilliant GP and really helped Nino to thrive despite his medical problems.

Children with Down syndrome are prone to problems due to low immunity and when I see youngsters with constant runny noses, watery eyes, ongoing coughs and repeated chest infections, I wish they had a GP like Nino had. Someone who could make such a difference to their wellbeing.

He became better and stronger and he's still on all the medication that she prescribed and has been since the age of seven. We have tried coming off it all at different times, but he always ends up with the watery eyes, runny nose and cough straight away. So, we are still on the medication which is fine because it works and keeps him well.

He's also allergic to strawberries (which is linked to a latex allergy) and this is such a shame because he loves them so much!

As a baby he was such a delight to be with, barely even cried and even with the therapies, he was always so content. I did lots of therapies on my own with him at home. I just did them and now they all have names, and the therapists recommend them. So, seems I was doing the right thing even when I didn't realise.

We did all sorts of things like hiding things in boxes for him to find as well as some physical stuff and I really enjoyed it. It was only me and him really for quite some time. His dad didn't really have a lot to do with him as he worked all day, so it was me and him doing intensive therapy at home for five years.

I tried to join some local groups because, even though I thoroughly enjoyed doing things with Nino, it was lonely. His dad worked a lot, my family were in Manchester and his dad's family spent half the year in Italy.

I was on my own an awful lot, but I'm independent and nothing ever stops me. I would make myself go places with him and always seemed to make friends along the way. Most people were kind and would sit with us, but some were unkind which was a little hard to take at times. He was always a delight and fun to be around, quite cheeky and has always had a wicked sense of humour.

Nino has also been diagnosed with epilepsy. He had a seizure at 14 but they didn't diagnose him at that stage. Apparently, you need to have more than one for them to diagnose epilepsy. He then had another major seizure at 21 which was when they diagnosed him, and he was given lifelong medication and an epilepsy care plan.

It hasn't been bad and has remained under control. He does have absences from time to time but apart from that, no major seizures. I'm hopeful he will continue that way now. He's amazing though, and anything that presents itself, he just takes in his stride.

Nothing ever seems to faze him at all. It's just something else that happens, he must take medication for it and then off he goes. This has slightly hindered his independence though because now he always must have someone with him, and he can't lock his bedroom door or the bathroom door just in case he has a seizure. We must be able to get to him quickly.

Nino, Aged 24 Years

So, the epilepsy nurses gave him all these rules to live by. He was going well with his independence and now he just needs to have support with him all the time.

He also has dysphasia which gives him a compromised swallow. He has choked quite a few times, and this has happened since his early teens. He was never really left on his own because of this so having someone be with him wherever he goes wasn't a major step and I don't think he really noticed. For me, it was just something we would have to have forever where I thought we would be able to stop the support once he became more independent.

He has a lovely girlfriend called Olivia. She is a little older than him, but they have been together for seven years and their relationship is just wonderful to watch. He went to a youth club one time and asked her to be his girlfriend. She said yes and they've been together ever since. He was very brave, and I was so proud of him.

He's always been an easygoing person and even when he was younger, it was wonderful seeing him reach his goals, even if they took longer to achieve. It never mattered. Even with walking, he was two before he walked. It was so cute because he walked in a circle for ages. He would move one foot and go around and around. Once he was three, he was walking most of the time.

We always went out and about and would catch the bus because I didn't have a car. We were so lucky where we lived because there were lots of parks, buses to catch from Bristol to the Harbour and plenty to see and do. I worked evenings, so I really loved going out during the day with him.

I enjoyed meeting all the other people because we never really had any support at all over the years. There was one place called Hop Skip Jump. It was a walk-in centre purpose-built for families with children with additional needs. Anyone could go at any time and mix with the other parents that were on a similar journey and siblings too.

There were staff that would take the children so you could go and enjoy a cuppa together and they had professionals come in to visit to help with questions and advice. That was the only place where I really joined a disability community. Unfortunately, it closed down some years later, but it really was a great place to meet and get support.

Occasionally I would contact the Down Syndrome Association here, but as I said earlier, I was in denial for a long time and I found it hard because once I opened up and said it, it made it real and then I would have to deal with it. I was trying to push away as much as I could and just get on with life.

Once I accepted everything, I did contact them and began receiving the magazines they send out and I spoke to people on their helplines from time to time. The online world has been great because I've been able to begin following many groups all over the world and it's really helped. I love sharing the things Nino gets up to and I love reading other people's stories.

So, early days, no support at all which was really my own doing but there wasn't a lot available. Now there are little groups that people can connect through, but it wasn't there when Nino was younger. I have many groups that I'm part of now and I've connected with many other parents, from all around the world. It's great to be able to make these connections now and see what everyone is up to.

Nino, Aged 24 Years

I love sharing what Nino is doing and since he left mainstream college, he's doing many things. He's a very busy young man. He's a signed model for Zebedee Talent and has been on TV, in magazines, on the catwalk, and part of exhibitions. He really loves doing this and the photos in his portfolio are amazing.

He loves his sport and is a rugby coach for the Bristol Bears Community Foundation and a football coach for Bristol City Robins Foundation. He's a goalkeeper for a local Mencap team. I love watching him play because of the passion he has for it, but struggle when he gets hit by the ball! He's also a competitive Special Olympic swimmer with The Bristol Sharks.

He is a trainee baker at the Stone Bakery, and he was working as an assistant in a local café. They recently laid him off for a few months because it's so quiet. They've told us it's very usual that they are quiet in the summer months and busier in the winter months. So, they've told him it's only temporary and he will be back in September.

His sister Lia is living with us, and she is one of his biggest fans and does some support with him. I work full time, so he needs the help while I'm not there. He's also got an assistant called Dean and he takes him to the gym, football and out socialising with his friends. Nino has a very busy social life and does so many things with his friends and girlfriend – movies, parties, dinners, golf, fitness, travel – and they all love seeing each other.

Nino has this amazing sense of knowing when people are not feeling right or if they are sad. He knows with me and will come up and put a hand on me to let me know he knows, no words just a look of complete unconditional true love. It's very interesting because even if I try and hide my feelings in front of him, he always knows when I'm not right and always comes to make sure I'll be okay.

He is a very determined young man and is always willing to give anything a go. He never gives up and his determination is phenomenal. He is very focused and knows exactly what he wants.

He's been learning a lot about his body, how it functions and what is good and bad for him. He's very focused on that and enjoys going to the gym to exercise and help with his health. Dean, his PA, takes him to the gym, and he has a great routine in place.

He strives to be very independent, but I have to guide him with that because of consequences. He doesn't really understand consequences from actions, so the safety element is still quite unknown. I have to tell him that being independent doesn't mean doing everything yourself, it means keeping safe and keeping others safe. Accepting support is key to being as independent as you can and it's okay if someone needs to help him, we all need some help sometimes.

He's a very laid-back person and really dislikes conflict. He doesn't like it at all when his friends have a falling out or raise their voices. It stresses him out and he gets anxious and worried. He would prefer for everyone to be comfortable and happy.

He's a very kind and generous young man with a very mischievous streak about him. He's got a cheeky twinkle in his eye and loves to irritate me. I don't mind because he gets it right back from me. I'll always ask if I'm irritating him and he will tell me yes, so I'll tell him to stop doing it to me. Always gives me a smile, so he knows exactly what he's doing. So cheeky!

Nino, Aged 24 Years

He's very thoughtful and loves to help me out if I need a hand. He loves to do things for me, and I always appreciate it. There's lots of love he has to give, to me and his sister, and I adore him.

I often explain his personality as glittery and shiny because there is this amazing presence he brings to a room. I'm so very proud of him and the way he carries himself. He has absolutely no judgement toward anyone and doesn't get fazed if he happens to meet a famous person. They are just a person like him and that's exactly how he treats them. He doesn't ever make a fuss, it's impossible to impress Nino, he is the most accepting human being I've ever met, such a beautiful soul with no game plan, no ulterior motive. Just open, honest and fully accepting of everyone.

He is not shy in expressing his opinion either. He was a VIP guest at a gala event by Bristol Sport Foundation, and he decided to tell the manager of Bristol City Football Club that they weren't doing well and needed him as a coach. He told him he needed to give him a job to help them and guess what? He got a job as an assistant football coach (his Bristol Bears Foundation manager also helped with this).

He formed a wonderful relationship with the manager from then on. He's been to training with the first team, had 1:1 goalkeeper training from the manager and coached other young players. He loves being a community rugby and football coach. He's in his element and has a great deal to offer.

He's a very sociable young man and whenever we go anywhere, he doesn't need me at all. He goes off and chats with everyone and loves making new friends. I watch him and wish more people were like him. I wish everyone looked at others like Nino does with no judgement. He just sees you for who you are. The only time I worry is if someone was to do him wrong and that's where the vulnerability is. I do worry about that a lot.

He has a great balance between the disability world and the typical world. They've both just intertwined organically for him and he's comfortable wherever he goes. I think his sister Lia has helped him with that by taking him out with her friends at times.

I think this is important because he has so much inclusion and acceptance around him. Inclusion to me means that everyone gets an opportunity to do what they would like to do, and they are treated with equity. So, not just the opportunity, but the tools, equipment, opportunities, training and support to be able to achieve their aspirations and goals in their lives.

The more society encourages equity, the more people will be comfortable with disability and diversity. No matter what limitations people may have, they still deserve an opportunity to give things a go, to be offered a chance. We are all living breathing human beings and we all deserve equal chances, equal opportunities, equal care, equal education – equality in all areas of life.

To me acceptance and inclusion goes hand in hand. With one, you have the other. It's understanding of others and knowing what's important. If you are like that, it dispels all the superficial things about life, the real truth and meaning of living becomes apparent and an inner peace can be achieved.

It's down to the bare bones of things. If you're a human being, it doesn't matter if you have pink skin, black skin, three arms, one leg, it really doesn't matter. Everyone has something to give, if they want to give it, and if they are offered the chance to give it. It's being kind and fair and allowing everyone to have their purpose in life, no level of judgement of that purpose, a purpose that's unique to an individual and what gives them contentment, equality, safety and happiness.

I really hope things become better and everyone can get the job they want, do the course they want, go out into the community without any worries at all. No judgement and nobody stopping anyone from at least giving things a try and getting support to try.

I've been very lucky with Nino and haven't faced too many obstacles over the years but there was one time when he was attending the private nursery opposite where we lived. They had a brilliant reputation, so I paid for him to attend from the age of three to five. There was no funding from the local authority, but suddenly at four years of age, they said they wanted him removed and to be placed in a mainstream nursery before he went to primary school.

He was thriving there, and he and I were so happy with the placement. I didn't want him to leave and go to another nursery before starting primary school. I had to put up a campaign with the nursery manager to make it possible for him to stay there. There was no reason why he couldn't go there – we lived across the road, we were paying the fees and he was doing so well.

We did want them to put in some specialist support to work with him in the private nursery setting. The idea was for the support staff to begin working with that member of staff and him and then pull away as he and they became more confident and learned more. They all knew him, and all really adored him, and they worked well with him. They were all learning sign language and were doing amazing things with him.

The local authority really didn't have a leg to stand on, but it was still a very difficult barrier to get through. It ended up giving the nursery manager the ability to give others the opportunity for their children to learn. Once Nino's case made it through and was put on a pilot for the support, it opened doors for others.

We haven't really faced any other obstacles because I've always armed myself well and because of the school I work at, I know a lot of the procedures and I know who to speak to so I can get the information I need.

Nino also has an amazing social worker. With Covid and other family issues, she has really been our rock and she advocates hard for Nino. I don't mind a challenge at times especially if it's for the rights of someone and she is the same as me. She fits in well with our family and works well with Nino.

It's important to look for the positives in everyone's personalities. Like the glitter and sparkle I see in Nino's personality and even though it's a bit of a challenge sometimes, it's who he is, and I never judge him or compare him to anyone else. Nobody should compare anyone against another. We are all our own particular genius.

Life with my boy hasn't been easy, it has been hard. But now, 24 years later, putting in all that hard work when he was young, all the time, effort and energy has paid off. His true personality really shines through now and to know he is happy, a productive member of our community, has a place in our community, has a purpose and a future filled with many more adventures, makes me so proud. I know it's been worth every sacrifice, every tear, every anxious moment, every fight, every moment of laughter and will always be that way.

Nino, Aged 24 Years

He has amazed me and continues to do so. All the challenges he has overcome has made him my hero. I am privileged that I gave birth to him, and every day is a pleasure with him. Even when he's being irritating and annoying, it's a pleasure to have him in my life and have him as my real-life hero.

He has made me a much better person in every way and reaches parts of my heart I never knew existed.

I'm in awe of the relationship between him and his sister Lia, and so very proud of the mutual adoration and sibling love that has grown between them from the day she was born 19 years ago. Such a privilege for me to be both their mum and to see their journey through life together.

I'm just so lucky to have my children and they will always be the greatest achievement of my life.

From the Hearts of Mums

From Nino ...

I do many things. I go to book club Monday, do swimming, community coach rugby and football, and play as a goalkeeper.

I work as a baker, and I have a girlfriend called Olivia. I asked her to be my girlfriend and she said yes. She has been my girlfriend for 7 years and she is older than me.

I am scared of big dogs and sometimes scared of little ones if they jump around too much.

I am a model, I love it.

I love fitness, sport, weightlifting, going to the gym, golf.

I eat healthy and drink lots of water.

I am great swimmer and love butterfly stroke best. I win trophies and gold medals and sometimes speeding tickets!

I go out with friends and my girlfriend to the cinema, bowling, sports, for meals, on holiday, boys nights, parties.

Love dancing and singing.

Like dressing smart, hair done nice and strong aftershave.

I love my life and like to tell other people about Down syndrome doesn't matter, do your best and live a happy life. Have fun and have friends.

Love my sister Lia and my mum Sharon.

Nino, Aged 24 Years

COURTNEY AND DI
Seaford, Melbourne, Australia

Courtney, Aged 27 Years

When Courtney was born, we had no idea that she had Down syndrome but when I think back, when I first looked at her, she didn't look how I expected our baby to look.

It was a very long labour (over 24 hours), and after Courtney was born and we were settled in our room, Brad went home for a sleep.

I remember looking at Courtney and just thinking that something didn't seem right. I asked the nurse if they would do some tests because of the feeling I had, because I wanted to find out if anything was going on with her.

I told her I wasn't sure exactly what I thought was going on, but I just didn't think she looked normal and how I expected her to look. They took her away and then came back with a doctor. He told me they had examined Courtney and could see a few characteristics of Down syndrome.

I lost my mind a little from that point and tried ringing Brad, but he was asleep. They put me in a private room and thankfully, Brad ended up coming in not long after that. I wasn't doing well with what I had been told and really needed him there.

It was an awful time to start with and when I think back now, I was grieving the loss of the child that I thought we were going to have. For at least one day the emotions were really ugly.

We had social workers, were seeing the paediatrician and at one point there was a psychologist that came in to see us. They sent in a few support people to help us as they could see we were really struggling.

Courtney, Aged 27 Years

They told us, even though Courtney had been born, we still had options. They told us we didn't have to keep the baby if we didn't want to and if we didn't think we could manage. I was astounded by this information and couldn't believe what they were saying to me. I didn't know what to say when they told us that.

I was breastfeeding Courtney, and I was bonding with her, and I couldn't even imagine giving her up. We were not coping well but I was starting to deal with it a lot quicker than Brad. Then we had one piece of advice that really helped.

We had some people we know come in to see us. They were really good friends of Brad's brother, and they have a son, Matt, who has Down syndrome. They brought us in this great book and the title was something like, *What Every Parent of a Child with Down Syndrome Should Read*.

They also told us it wasn't the end of the world. Matt was three at the time and was doing well. They looked at Courtney and told us how beautiful they thought she was and that everything would be okay. Matt's mum Jen also told me we will have a normal life and we will be a normal family.

We were getting there slowly but I remember this family helped so much. When we checked out of the hospital, before we left, the paediatrician came over to do a check on Courtney. He was listening to her heart when he told us she had a hole in her heart.

All I could think was, 'What else is going to go wrong?' We had to go to the Royal Children's Hospital, and it was Christmas Eve. All we wanted to do was go home and see our family for Christmas. While we were there, we met other families and started talking. When they asked what we were there for with

Courtney and we told them she had Down syndrome and had a hole in her heart, their response was, 'Oh, is that all'.

For us it was huge, but some of these families had children in there with a terminal illness or waiting for a heart transplant. So, I guess they knew what we were dealing with would be able to be sorted quickly once we saw the specialists. We didn't know that though and everything we were being told was so unexpected.

We were in the cardiac ward, and it was right on Christmas time. When we went in to see the doctors, we were told they couldn't do anything for Courtney right away. We wanted to go home for Christmas, and it was great that we could do that to get our girl home and enjoy spending some time away from hospital.

This five days in hospital was tough because we went from thinking we were going down one route with our first child, to a completely different one full of the unknown. We didn't have the internet to search information and only had books to read. There wasn't really a lot of information available.

Always questioning whether she would be able to talk, walk, what supports would she need, will she ultimately be able to live independently and many different things like that going through our minds.

Now, at 27, we just want Courtney to be happy and healthy and be able to live her best life. So far, she is doing that, and we love watching her thrive. She has great activities she is doing and has a wonderful social life.

When we are out and about and people stare, I often wonder why they are staring. It's mainly younger and older people that seem to do it and I don't think they're staring with any negative thoughts. Sometimes I think they look because they may know someone with Down syndrome.

When she was younger, I would find myself staring at older people with Down syndrome because I was curious. We were at the beginning of our journey and were heading to where they were, so I just wanted to see what they were doing. I really think curiosity is a big reason why people stare.

So, we were able to enjoy Christmas at home but we were straight back to the Royal Children's Hospital after Christmas so they could do the testing they needed to do. Courtney had to have surgery because she had several holes in her heart and had to have a catheter test initially to see how big they were. She was 3.6kg born and she needed to weigh 4.0kg before they would perform the open heart surgery and it took four months for her to gain 400grams.

The medical staff we had were very supportive when Courtney was born and through all the extra things we had to go back for. We had a paediatrician that we saw for a while before he retired. We also had a wonderful midwife who was amazing with us and really helped me with breastfeeding.

She was extremely patient, and I ended up being able to breastfeed Courtney for six months. She was beautiful with me and Courtney, and it was great to have someone like her while we were going through all the emotions. I didn't really expect any different because they've done all the training and I'm sure would have dealt with other families with children with Down syndrome.

They were probably the only two that were supportive and caring with us though even though I did think everyone should be. The rest didn't really handle things well. They did put us in a private room and made us comfortable, but it would have been nice for someone to come and sit with us and just answer some questions and be there for us.

It would have been good because we asked our friends not to come in as I just didn't feel up to it. My girlfriends all wanted to come in and they didn't know why I didn't want them to or what the problem was. I just didn't want to talk to anyone, and it was only immediate family that came in. Our parents came in and it was difficult for them to process everything as well.

Supports were hard to find, and we didn't really find any. We did get told about Biala which was early intervention and Courtney was able to start when she was quite young. I don't remember where we found out about Biala and to be honest I was probably depressed for the first 12 months after Courtney was born. I recognise that now, but at the time I think I was just going through the motions and doing the best I could. Sometimes I felt as though I was on autopilot.

I remember there were not many supports or information and nobody really told us anything. We had people like social workers come to see us but no advice about early intervention or anything like that was given.

The supports we had were from family. My mum had me when she was young, so we are close in age and when she came in, she was very positive and told us how beautiful Courtney was. She wasn't worried about the Down syndrome diagnosis at all.

Courtney, Aged 27 Years

In fact, she just said 'Down syndrome, blah, blah, blah'. She was so very happy to have a granddaughter to love.

When we told her the staff had said we didn't have to keep her, my Mum was in shock. She said, 'Oh my God, you can't do that'. She said if we were thinking about that, she would take Courtney and she would look after her. I calmed her down and told her we were not giving her up, and that I was just telling her what we had been told.

Both our families were amazing. They all loved her right from the start and were not fazed by the Down syndrome diagnosis at all. They loved her for exactly who she is and have always been there for us.

Our friends were the same and so supportive. A lot of my girlfriends I had back then, are still my friends now. They were all great because if they didn't know something, they would just ask. They didn't pussyfoot around and knew they could be honest with us. It was great to have them by our side, especially in the early days.

My best friend's daughter was around 12 when Courtney was born so, has known her all her life. When she got married, she had Courtney in her bridal party which was so special. They've always been fully accepting and loved her for who she is.

We attended Biala for a little while and then we found a place called Epic. Again, I don't remember how we found out about that. They were incredible there and it was run by a husband and wife. Biala was about physio and speech, but at Epic they were teaching Courtney how to read.

It was incredible. This was all before school with Courtney attending between the age of three and four. It was a kind of speech therapy, but they were incorporating language and reading as well as teaching her shapes and other things like that. It was almost like preschool.

They helped me with other things with Courtney as well. One day, when we were there, she said to Courtney, 'You still wearing a nappy?' She turned to me and asked me when I was going to get her out of the nappy. I was pregnant with Jack at the time so she said it would be best to get Courtney toilet trained before the baby arrived.

She told me there was nothing stopping me from toilet training her and that Courtney would be very capable. She told me I could do this and gave me such confidence. She said the sky's the limit, don't set the bar down low, you can do anything with her. They pushed us but not in a way that was terrifying, it was all just so supportive.

We met some other families at Epic, and this was great for us too. Meeting people travelling on the same road is always a good thing as you can support each other while you are all going through the same things with your children.

We got through things quite well but as time has gone on, it's great for new parents because there's more awareness now and much more education around inclusion and educating the wider public. More resources are available and if you aren't told about things, you are able to search on the internet now.

The education around Down syndrome itself is much better than it was. Being able to show people that Courtney and all her friends are all different like everyone else. They have their own personalities, they're not always happy, they do go through all the different emotions like we all do. Don't try to fit them in a box because they are not all the same.

We did private speech for a while too as the people at Epic were very big on everything to do with the tongue and lips. People with Down syndrome can have a protruding tongue, so we worked very hard on this with Courtney. Always working on putting the tongue back in and closing her lips. When you work on things like this, you can make a change.

She didn't really enjoy speech therapy and I think that was because there was so much of it. We did it at early intervention and then the private speech therapist. I think Courtney found it hard, so she didn't enjoy it and I'm sure there were times she didn't want to do it. Bad luck, I always said, it needs to be done.

She's never loved walking either, so I don't think she enjoyed the physical therapy much. But it's important for the exercise to be there just as it is for everyone else. Weight gain can be common in people with Down syndrome, so it's extremely important to keep on top of all of that.

Even now she doesn't like the exercise or walking, and she will even cry and tell me she doesn't want to go. I always tell her it's important and remind her that the doctor said if she doesn't keep moving, she will lose her strength and maybe end up in a wheelchair. I know she doesn't want that to happen.

Now she does dance classes and Pilates. The Pilates started after she broke her ankle as it was a good exercise for her to keep her muscles strong so she could recover well from the fracture. She still does it now and both these things are something she enjoys so much. It's not a struggle to get her to these activities at all.

With her classes at BAM, her dance group, they also do yoga and fitness. She loves the yoga but still doesn't enjoy the fitness side of it, but it's important for her to keep active, so she goes. Plus, her friends are there doing the same thing and that's a good motivator for her.

Her classes at BAM are awesome because she really loves all of that. She loves to dance and sing and do anything theatrical. BAM is her life where all her friends go and it's a great social outlet for her too.

She loves the theatre and movies, loves to dress up and get her nails and hair done. She really loves all the girly stuff. When we were getting ready for the BAM concert, it was everything, the hair, makeup, nails, and she felt like a million bucks once it was all done.

One of her favourite things of all is the socialising with all her friends. She loves to go out with them and just be with her group like we all do. I love seeing her with her friends and hearing about all the things they get up to. When she was first born, I didn't know if this would be something she would be able to enjoy, but she has a better social life than the rest of us.

It's also great because a few years ago Courtney was very quiet and shy but as she has become older and started getting more involved with BAM she has really come out of her shell. She loves to perform on stage in their concerts and recently we were at a local market where some of the students sang to the crowd.

Courtney, Aged 27 Years

A few years ago, Courtney would never have done that, but she loved it and gave it her all.

With all of this, Courtney is now very confident, and she is a very funny young lady. She is very honest, and she will tell you how it is. No sugar coating of anything and I think we should all be more like that.

She can still be a little shy, but when she is with her crew, the confidence just pours out of her. It's beautiful to watch because you can see the love that she has for her friends and vice versa. She is part of a group called Wildcats and they are so tight. Their friendship is unconditional and they all watch out for each other.

Her speech now has come such a long way and we don't go to therapy anymore. I think all the drama and other activities she does with BAM has helped with that. She is also a great reader, and she does quite well with her spelling, but predictive text has helped with that. Because of that she can send messages to her friends, and she can interact with them on social media like we all do.

We are extremely proud of Courtney, and I want her to be able to go out and about in the community without having to worry. I want her to be herself without being judged. Sometimes we must be careful how we interpret others as well because at times it is just curiosity and not judgement.

There are a lot of people who haven't had Down syndrome in their lives, so they are curious, and I would love people to come and ask questions if they want to know something.

Sometimes though there is judgement, and I would love it if we could eliminate that. I don't think Courtney pays any attention to any of it, but we see it and it does hurt sometimes. I would just like people to think and be kinder toward others.

It's a lot better today than it was 20 years ago and I do think people are more aware. You can definitely see more kindness toward people with disabilities, but the education is still important and needs to be shared.

I think people with Down syndrome and people with other disabilities are more accepted and included than they were many years ago and it's great because it enables them to do the things they love, and we don't have to worry as much.

We enrolled Courtney in mainstream school when she was five and the school was great. They really guided us along and let us know when it was becoming time for her to move to a more supported environment.

She has more choice now especially with the NDIS. So, if we want to go on a holiday and she doesn't want to come with us, she doesn't have to anymore. She is in her late twenties and like any other person of that age, doesn't always want to go with Mum and Dad. We can set things up so she can stay home and that way she is much happier because she can keep doing all her activities and going out with her friends and we can enjoy our holiday.

She's an adult now and wants to make her own choices and this can happen because of what is happening today. It's great and it gives her more confidence and allows her to have her own voice with what she wants to do.

Courtney, Aged 27 Years

At times we will go with her to some of her events like the Rampage Radio Show they are doing now with BAM. Sometimes what they are doing is a fundraiser and it's local radio so it's awesome to be able to support her with that as well as supporting our local community.

If we don't want to go with her, we don't have to, and this is also great because the whole family can have a choice in what we do. She can go to these events without us because she is surrounded by her friends and teachers and it's a very safe environment.

There are still people that I think need more education. Recently, I saw a woman push past Courtney and her friend Charli without even thinking about how that would make them feel. I did stand up for the girls and said something. With or without a disability, behaviour like that is extremely rude and people shouldn't do it.

I do worry about when things like that happen and there is nobody there to advocate for them. What happens? People just really need to be kinder I think and respect others. We are all people, and we all have the same rights.

Courtney is a real homebody and loves being at home with us. I worry about when she may like to move out of home because some of her friends have already done this. I worry because I don't know who will advocate for her and who is going to help her with personal care. Others don't love her like I do, and I am concerned about what will happen in the future.

I know the people that work in supported housing are amazing, but they're not her mum. Will they care for her the same way I do? Will she be happy, and will she be able to be heard if something isn't right? I know they care for their clients, but to me, it's just not the same.

We've asked her what she thinks about moving out of home and it's just not something she is thinking about at all. We asked her if she thought she may move out when she's 30 and it was a flat no.

I do worry about the future for Courtney, and I would love to see change in the awareness and education for others so there is more acceptance. We live in the world of disability and are accepting and inclusive and we do hear her and what she wants to do.

But this doesn't happen in the wider community as much as it should. I would like to see this changed and for Courtney to be seen as a person first, because that is what she is. She is just like you and me even though she may look a little different. We are all different.

This acceptance isn't just limited to people with disabilities, it should be for everyone no matter who you are. Really, just being kind and seeing that we all have the right to do what we want to do and live our lives to the fullest.

Parents should educate their children about disability because they will come across many who live with it within the wider community. There isn't many children living with disability in the mainstream school setting, so not all children are exposed or have a good understanding. Today, we see more stories on social media, but there is still an understanding that needs to go with that.

It's okay to say hello or smile. I say hello to people all the time when I'm out in the community and I know a lot of others do too. So, you should still do this if you pass by someone with a disability. They will say hi back.

Courtney is an amazing young lady, and we are so proud of her. She has an amazing memory which blows my mind. She recalls things from holidays so precisely that we have long forgotten about. I'm talking holidays she went on when she was three.

Nobody should ever think that just because she has Down syndrome, she is not smart. She understands and takes everything in, and she learns from everything. With technology she is super smart and can do anything on any device. Much better than me.

She's our daughter and we have always wanted the very best for her. I would love it if everyone could see what we see when we look at her.

'Love the life you live.'
Bob Marley

From the Hearts of Mums

DOUG AND BONNIE
Santa Maria, California, USA

Doug, Aged 73
(14 February 1948 – 1 August 2021)

From the Hearts of Mums

*Sometimes the family we have in our lives are chosen family.
A friend can be a mother figure in someone's life with the same love.
Doug and Bonnie's story is a wonderful, unique story of chosen family,
friendship, love and support.*

I first met Doug and his family when I was hired as a behaviour modification program instructor. This means that my group were the individuals that had difficult behaviours when out in the community.

It was my job to try and retrain and use reinforcers to tone down the behaviours so they could be more acceptable in the community. I started working at VTC in 1992 and this is the year I met Doug. He didn't become part of my group until 1994.

I had changed job sites and I would usually have three to four individuals in my group. Doug was added to the group, and I did know who he was but didn't know much about him. His family are quite famous at VTC because they were instrumental in creating the program in the first place. It's a huge program and very well known.

I was told Doug was joining the group and I received his case file. He had many behaviours for me to work on and most of it was hoarding, trash collecting and what they called eloping which is also known as absconding. It was quite silly, but he would just leave the group randomly and walk off.

I received a call from Mr McLain, Doug's father saying he wanted to meet me. I had never had a parent ask to meet me before, but I decided it would be okay. Most of the people I worked with came from group homes and there was never any parent involvement with me as a worker.

Doug, Aged 73 (14 February 1948 - 1 August 2021)

When I met him, I was taken aback at first because he was a very small man. I am quite tall, and I guess I just expected him to be tall as well.

He wanted to meet with me to ask me what it was I thought I could do for his son. Nobody had ever asked me that question before, but I responded by telling him I was hoping to get him to behave better when in the community. I told him I would work hard, and we would see what happens.

As time went along, I got invited to their house to have coffee and get to know them better. I believe I was the first worker/instructor that was allowed to come into the house and see the natural environment of one of my clients.

Even the behavioural interventionist and the people that were creating behavioural plans only ever had a brief look into the home, so it was very interesting.

So first it was Doug that I met and then his family and boy did they give me the best cup of coffee I've ever had. It was from Brazil, and I was zooming all over the place. I felt an instant connection with them, and I knew straight away they were going to be a family that would be part of my life.

When I began working with Doug, we had a job site at the Court House that was a little sandwich area that sold snacks and sandwiches for the jurors. I had to always keep an eye on Doug because he would sneak around the garbage dumpsters and collect garbage that he would then hide in the bushes.

I knew what he was up to so I would walk around to the bushes and ask him if the garbage was his. He would always tell me no very adamantly because he knew he shouldn't be doing it.

I would be very elaborate and start throwing it behind me to put it back in the dumpster and he would get so mad with me. It was an ongoing saga with the garbage, but I never stopped persisting with him.

He was also very well known in the community, and he got away with things that most people wouldn't get away with. He would steal from the stores and because he knew the owners, he would get away with it. They would always say, 'He didn't mean to steal it.' I would immediately respond with, 'Are you crazy?' Of course, he meant it. He knew exactly what he was doing.

In my job, we did a lot of integration. So, we had the lunch area, we would go to the library, go to the bank and they would all earn a pay check. Doug had the money to purchase things from the stores, but he never really understood the value of money which I think was why he always stole from the stores.

I would start getting him to use his money to buy things in the stores and pay for the things he was trying to steal. Explaining to him that it wasn't his to take and that he had money in his pocket to buy it if he really wanted it.

His pockets were always full of change. In fact, Doug used to walk around with about 12 lbs of stuff in all of his pockets. So, as well as his behaviours, we had that to deal with and try to sort out with him.

He was also very cheeky. We would be out in the community, trying to make sure he would stay with the group, and he would

Doug. Aged 73 (14 February 1948 - 1 August 2021)

be causing mayhem by being interruptive to the other clients. He would be behind my back and start poking the other clients. It would drive them mad, and they would get so angry. He would always say he wasn't doing anything. Very cheeky man Mr Doug.

As I got to know Doug's family, I asked if I could take him out to do things separately from the group. So, one to one trips with me out and about in the community. I knew it would be a good break for his mum and dad. His mum was 94 and she had just had a health episode and was now set up downstairs in the house. It was a two-story house, and she couldn't manage the stairs anymore.

So that meant Doug had free reign of the upstairs part of the house, and he was a hoarder. He had hoarded 2 full bedrooms of stuff to the ceiling. Everything from pieces of paper to giant cement boulders that he had found from construction work. He hoarded all sorts of materials that had been tossed in the garbage. He kept bread wrappers and would layer napkins on his bed.

He had layers and layers of trash and then he would methodically take a few things out to the dumpster and then bring a bunch of other stuff back in. He would sneak out in the middle of the night to collect the big stuff and he would go into people's yards in the neighbourhood and take stuff.

I was trying really hard to figure out how I could help with all of this, and it wasn't coming any time soon. I was able to use our trips out as a reinforcer for good behaviour. I would tell him if he wanted to come out with me, he would have to make sure he didn't take anything, not to steal and to use his own money. If he didn't listen, we wouldn't go out and he didn't like that.

That's how the relationship with me, Doug and his family began, and I really enjoyed our days out together. I loved working with Doug. He was frustrating, that's for sure because he kept getting away with things. If he got caught, he would deny it.

He never thought it was a big deal because everyone always let him get away with things and would say he didn't mean it, or he was just messing around. I used to say to them, 'So, I can steal something from your store and it's not a big deal?' Of course, they didn't agree with that, so I was trying to show them it was no different with Doug.

I even introduced him to a police officer so he could talk to Doug about what happens when you steal from others. He said to Doug, 'I hear you have sticky fingers.' Doug was funny because he didn't understand sarcasm and would tell the officer that his hands are clean.

We ended up taking Doug and the whole group for a tour of the jail cells at the Court House. I told them this is where people go when they take things they shouldn't, and when they break the law. Doug didn't see it as a big deal until I told him there was no television and no coffee. Then he would tell me, 'Oh no, I don't like that, I can't do that.' The thought of no television or coffee definitely wasn't something Doug would cope with.

Things were starting to click but I would always bust him with things in his pockets from stores. I would tell him every time, 'Doug, nothing in your pockets.' He would tell me okay, and say not with you, only with father. He even used to take the sensor tags, so we would be walking out of the store and all the alarms would start going off.

Doug. Aged 73 (14 February 1948 - 1 August 2021)

It was so embarrassing, but I would always take him back and make him accountable. He never thought it was a big deal, and sometimes he would even steal the things back from me that I had taken from him to return to the store.

Finally, one store manager said, 'I'm done with dealing with this, you can't come in here anymore.' Doug of course, didn't believe it so I talked to my supervisors and asked for someone else to come with me. Doug needed to understand that this was not okay.

We had to come up with a plan because nobody had ever followed through with consequences for him. So, I took my group to the store and when Doug went to go in, I told him he couldn't go in. The store manager won't let you come back because you keep taking his stuff.

Finally, success! Doug started saying, 'I can't do that.' The need to steal for him was very strong and was like an obsession. And it was anything, he would take things like women's make up containers, so I used to tell him it was for a girl and that he took girl's stuff. 'Oh, I can't do that,' he would say and then he would put it back. Mind you, he would have 10 other things as well.

He was very cute, well known in the community and one of the first participants with the VTC so he was almost very famous in that environment. Very hard to try and work on his behaviours, but I was not going to give up.

The VTC program was developed initially by a group of families with children with additional needs. They could see they needed something more for their children and once it was developed, it just took off from there.

Once Doug and I had developed a good relationship we started taking him on vacations and stays at our house to give his parents a break. His mum had passed when we were away with Doug on a cruise. She was in hospital while we were away and when we returned, she had passed. Doug spent more time with me during this difficult time. It was after this that the discussion of Doug coming to live with us started.

His dad knew he couldn't keep looking after him as he was ageing, and he was worried about Doug being put into a group home. Doug would not cope with it at all for many reasons including having trouble with self-care. He had also gained a lot of weight and needed good one to one care.

His dad expressed his worry and not knowing what to do. I told him that my husband and I hoped he would come and live with us. His dad was so emotional and grateful. I didn't realise that it was such a big deal. I'm not a parent of a person with a disability and didn't realise the worry that came with it about when they would pass away. What would happen to their child?

He told me they had a strong faith that someone would come along one day, and I guess it was me and my husband. His dad used to call me the mover and shaker. He said I always got things done.

So, we started slowly progressing and talking about Doug coming to live with us. Doug loved being at our house because we had television and he could watch his favourite shows. We would set up a small shed for him, so he had a place for all the things he collected. It was also a place where he could go and do his nonsense and not get in trouble.

Doug, Aged 73 (14 February 1948 - 1 August 2021)

The shed would get cleaned out every once in a while, but it was his safe place along with his bedroom. He needed space like we all do where he could go through his stuff and if he wanted to break something in there he could because they were his things. He would break things when he was angry, and he would slam doors and cuss like a sailor.

Doug moved in with us in 2000 and it was quite a funny time because my mum had been living with us and she had to move out now. So, I was moving her out and moving Doug in. I had everything ready, and we set a date. He was quite used to staying with us by this time because he used to stay for a week at a time.

The day I went to pick Doug up, his dad went to get his bag. He thought he was just coming out for the day. He had forgotten. 'Today is moving in day,' I said. 'Oh!' he replied, 'is that today?'

Before we left, I asked Doug if was sure he wanted to come live with us. He told me he was sure as long as he could come visit his father. Of course, we were going to do that, but it didn't last too long. We only visited a few times because it was too hard on them both. Doug was torn between the new home and his old home.

He liked the new home environment where he had different freedom and a television. Dad was older and the whole thing was to help him and give him the peace of mind that Doug was going to be cared for and be safe. He passed away just shy of his 100th birthday.

Mind you, when he was 98, he was still out riding horses while Doug was living with me. He got to go and do the things he loved and remembered from when he was growing up. He was able to go to church retreats and when Doug was with him, he couldn't do that. It was important for him so I'm glad we were able to make that possible for him.

That is how he came to live with us. I was already handling all of his medical things because his parents didn't know Doug's insurance covered the cost of it all and the appointments. Doug had awful healthcare access, but it wasn't from them not wanting to help him. They just didn't know that they could. They would pay cash for his medications for all those years and when I came along, I showed them the right way to do it, so it didn't cost them anything.

They really had no idea of what benefits they could get with Doug's medical. They would talk about not being able to receive it forever but that didn't make sense to me because if you have a long-term illness, injury, or disease, it has to be managed. Because they were always paying cash, there was never any follow-up medically.

When my husband and I were holidaying in Tahiti just before Doug moved in, I had a dream that he was in hospital after suffering a heart attack. When we came home, Doug was in the hospital, but he had a fall. He had a blood clot in his leg and couldn't walk. He was up to no good and was climbing a neighbour's fence when he fell off. His father had to bring him into the house on a dolly.

None of the health care professionals wanted to help him or fix his knee or leg. Blood clot and torn meniscus and they didn't want to help him. Needless to say, when we returned from holiday, I expressed my dissatisfaction. It was unacceptable. He had been dancing at a party the week before. But they didn't think he would cope with the surgery and corrective treatments.

Doug, Aged 73 (14 February 1948 - 1 August 2021)

His father allowed me to assist with medical needs. We were able to change his primary care doctor. They were fantastic and listened to us and what would be best for Doug. They got him on the right track, and we were able to get Doug into physical therapy. It took a year, but he went from a wheelchair and not walking at all, to walking normally. They thought he would need a knee brace forever, but he was able to stop wearing it.

The physical therapy was great, and Doug enjoyed it. He was able to play his guitar, he made friends, and they had coffee. They would use the coffee as a reward for him if he tried walking. Worked very well.

From that point was when I became heavily involved in Doug's medical affairs apart from just the medication. I couldn't believe they thought he wouldn't cope just because he had Down syndrome. I wrote advocacy letters (handwritten) to the doctors as well as the American Medical Association and told them how Doug had been mistreated. He should have been given the opportunity from the beginning for treatment and therapy. Thankfully, as I mentioned above, it all got sorted out and Doug received the care he needed.

His dad didn't mind me taking over the medical and was quite relieved. The whole family were relieved because they knew I would advocate heavily for Doug. Becoming family with Doug seemed to just happen and it was as though it was always meant to be. Doug living with us was fantastic and I was so pleased we could help.

Doug had sensory issues, but it was about getting dirty. Like when kids fall over, and they get their hands dirty. Doug would never allow himself to fall down and get dirty, but he would wear dirty clothing. And if he took a washcloth to himself he thought that was it ... he was clean. And if you let him get away with it, he would wear the same clothes for days.

But the biggest thing was about getting things in his pocket. He would be looking at you straight in the face while you wiped your face with a napkin, and somehow while you were looking at him, he would grab it and put it in his pocket.

It was always very thought out and something he would be thinking about and planning all day. Taking other people's things was also big for Doug and I spent all my time telling them how this was not a good thing. Just because he's a cute little man, it's not okay for him to do that. He understands right from wrong. It was always a battle to get people to treat him and the other clients just like everyone else.

He would also wear layers and layers of clothing and sometimes he would tie something tightly around his waist. He would wear a tight belt and hang things from it. One of the layers of clothing used to be his mother's pyjama bottoms because they felt so nice on his skin. And then he would layer more clothing on top of that. It was a big deal for him and very hard for me to modify.

We would compromise and it would be okay to do that at home but when he was out with the group working, he had to be safe. His clothing had to be clean. He loved wearing button up shirts and they were long. One time, on the job site, he came out and had poop on the back of the shirt. I made him go and get cleaned up and he was so mad. He came out of the bathroom and handed me this strap he had stolen from one of the baseball players. It was endless.

Doug. Aged 73 (14 February 1948 - 1 August 2021)

He didn't like being cold and was never just in a t-shirt and shorts, even in the hot weather. I'm not really sure if he liked the feeling of the heat and that is why he wore so many layers or if he just liked the feeling of those layers of clothes on his body.

He also had a very high tolerance to pain. I wouldn't even know he was in pain until I had to micromanage his behaviours. Every once in a while, he would come up and show me something that clearly needed attention long before he showed me.

He came up and showed me his thumb one day and said, 'What are you going to do about that?' It was so swollen, and it had an abscess on it so guess where we went. The doctor. It seems he got a splinter in it. So, we head to the emergency department.

Another time, Doug developed a rash on his back. The doctor said it was allergies and we put cream on it and gave him allergy pills. This rash wouldn't go away. His fingers became swollen, and the emergency doctor said it was dermatitis. More cream. Another doctor appointment and me begging for him to be seen by a skin specialist. He had developed this horrendous rash all over him. I was so shocked as I was always super hypervigilant with him.

We had to wait for a referral to a dermatologist because of the health care system over here, they couldn't help us with the rash at the hospital. After three months and wrong diagnoses, he was sent to a dermatologist specialist. As soon as he saw Doug, he put him into quarantine because he had what was called 'Norwegian scabies'. I was mortified.

I can't imagine how uncomfortable he must have been because it was all over his body and trying to sleep would have been impossible with all the itching. We named it itchy, and I told him he got it from digging in the garbage. I asked him if he wanted itches and he told me 'Oh heck, no way.' I thought that may stop the hoarding, but no.

There are so many medical stories I could share about Doug because of his high threshold for pain. If he had a belly pain, he wouldn't walk. He would just sit there. And if it was chronic pain, he would be happy to sit there because it wouldn't hurt if he didn't move. I had to really keep a close eye on him and learn about all the different things he would do rather than tell me something was hurting.

Doug had been diagnosed with chronic leukemia and had been going to a haematologist for it to be monitored. So, we were watching for anything like runny nose, cough, cold or flu because if he contracted anything like that we would have to go straight to emergency.

So, in 2020, when the pandemic of COVID-19 hit, we were very vigilant in keeping him safe and away from anyone that would possibly pass on the virus to him. It was very traumatic, and I had to give up my life to stay home with him because he was immune compromised. We couldn't have anyone over, and I was very overprotective of him. In the beginning, there was no lockdown yet, but we were staying at home.

It was hard for Doug because he didn't understand why he couldn't go to his program. They tried to be creative and come up with things for us to do at home, but it was difficult for him. He's a real people person and loves to hug which made me even more protective of him in keeping people away.

Doug, Aged 73 (14 February 1948 - 1 August 2021)

He was getting bored and began sitting on the front porch waiting for the mail carrier. He enjoyed it when he came to deliver mail and loved it if there was something for him. So, I decided to ask family and friends to send him something in the mail. Just a letter or card, but something for him.

Something exciting for him to look forward to. Once the official lockdowns began to happen, my husband was still able to work, so it was just me and Doug at home and he was getting very bored and depressed. Not like him at all. He kept asking what we were going to do, telling me he needed to go to work and would ask me when we are going out. He had been going to the program since he was in his twenties and now he was 72.

So, I put a post on Facebook asking friends and family to send a letter or card to him. I tried to schedule it so something would arrive each day. It was so funny because I wanted to make sure he had something to look forward to every day.

Within an hour of putting the post up, I had filled the first month for mail to arrive. Within two to three hours, I had friends of friends and family of family contacting me telling me what a good idea it was, and they would send him something. I broke down sobbing because I felt a little overwhelmed by it all but also so grateful by people's generosity.

I couldn't believe all these people wanted to send something to Doug. But, when I think about it now, they were stuck at home too, so it was easy for them to sit down and write a letter or card and send it. Something for them to do as well.

He started getting letters in the mail and then one of my friends sent him some facial creams and he thought that was very cool.

He didn't know why people were sending him things, especially the people he didn't know, so I decided to record us opening the mail to post on Facebook to say thank you to everyone.

After a few days he had something like 30 letters come in the mail. What was happening? And then we started receiving things from around the world. People were sharing the post and making the call out themselves and it went viral. My husband told me to spread them out so there wasn't too many to open at once. But I couldn't do that as he had the same rights as us to see his mail. It's important for everyone to be treated the same and be given the same rights.

So, we recorded it and posted it on Facebook. Doug would love watching it back before I put it up and people were really enjoying their daily 'Mail Call'. We received such a lovely warm response from it all.

I had to be careful and really watch him because he would watch me open the letters and packages and I could see he was eyeing off the rubbish. I would have to quickly put it in a spot where he wouldn't notice it and then get rid of it as soon as we were finished.

When he would watch himself back on the recording, he would talk to himself and say, 'Look at Doug', 'Why does he do that?' He'd say, 'Look at all that mess and all those letters.' It was interesting to watch him observing himself and looking at the way he was acting. For him it was like watching a movie but with him in it, and he loved to see himself.

Once we could go out a little, the ritual was to get the mail, do the recording and go for a drive for coffee. Some days I wouldn't

Doug, Aged 73 (14 February 1948 - 1 August 2021)

feel like doing the mail and recording but Doug really looked forward to it. If I told him not now, he would say 'Well, I can't stand it, you better change your mind.' How could I resist that?

Whenever we finished 'Mail Call', it was always so good and so much fun for both of us. It was a wonderful thing and so simple to do. We have made so many connections around the world now. Doug is an ambassador for Making Chromosome Count, and we have made lovely friends in Australia.

I even won a virtual party for Doug from a group in Australia called Friend In Me. It was an online party on Zoom with superheroes and music and dancing. It was amazing. He enjoyed it but didn't have a clue about what it was, and it was hard to explain that these people were from the other side of the world. Such a new concept for him.

People also started sending me messages asking me questions. One of the questions was 'How did you get him to stay alive?' They asked that because he was the oldest person living with Down syndrome living independently in a supported situation. Others that were older were living in either a group home or extended care home. They weren't renting a room and having a family life with their roommates.

That was another time when I realised how unique our situation was, and I began to realise why people thought it was so special. It was never out of the ordinary for me because Doug was always going to be our family. I couldn't have children and my purpose was Doug. It was normal for us.

After some time, the mail would slow down a little. All I had to do was tell people on the video that it had slowed down and

Doug was a little disappointed and BOOM! The mail would start rolling in again.

It was interesting trying to explain to Doug that mail was coming from all over the world. He didn't really have a concept of that. His family had taken him on many trips around America but trying to make sense to him over people thousands of miles away was difficult. I would tell him where something was from and he would say 'oh yeah', but he didn't really understand. We had received a map and the idea was to pinpoint where everything had come from to give him an idea.

One of the things I struggled with for a while was when people would praise me for looking after Doug. You know, they would say, 'There's a special place in heaven for you.' I really didn't understand it because Doug was part of us. He was our friend, and he was our family, so having him live with us really was a no brainer.

When I spoke with my friend Julie in Australia, she told me that as soon as Darcy was born, she immediately began to worry about what was going to happen to him when she and her husband weren't there anymore. Who would help him? Where would he live? I had never thought about it like that. And when she said all of that, I could see where she was coming from and why everyone had put me on this pedestal.

Before we moved Doug in with us, we were thinking about doing a group home situation but found out there were too many restrictions and licensing, and it wouldn't have kept it as a family environment. We wanted to keep a safe and loving family environment. The legalities of getting Doug to live with us were huge because we weren't his blood family. It was illegal

Doug. Aged 73 (14 February 1948 - 1 August 2021)

for people to have someone with a disability living in their home without some sort of agency or certification.

We really had to fight to have him live with us. It was interesting because the agencies we were fighting didn't know how to respond because it had never happened before. We were supposed to keep everything confidential from the family but that didn't sit right with me. We were discussing and making plans for their son, their brother and I wanted them to know what was being said and what was going on.

I ended up telling his family what was going on and soon I became the difficult one. But I didn't care because the family had a right to know, and Doug had a right to choose where he was going to live. I also had departmental and developmental services coming into my home telling me I was doing things wrong. I didn't know what that meant because I monitored everything really carefully and kept books. The supervisor took the books for two weeks and when they came back, she said they were fine and up to date. The agency found a medication error and I was sanctioned. I thought they would shut me down. I was mortified.

We couldn't have others come and stay with Doug, be with him or help us unless they were employees of this particular agency. My hands were tied, but I did organise in secret for friends to meet him at the bus if I was running late and other things like that. For me, it was not normal to not be able to have someone that loves him come and be with him.

That agency did get us started and I was grateful to have had everything in place to do it without them. It was very money-driven and they got paid to come and oversee me with Doug.

I used that as ammunition to advocate that it would cost a lot less for us to support Doug than it is to pay for this agency. All his social security money was going to this agency. They were getting almost $5,000 a month. And we were getting $1,300 a month that was meant to cover food, rent and everything else plus the 24-hour care. We didn't expect a lot of money because we were doing it anyway, but it was the whole point of it.

I ended up getting the governing agency to have a family meeting to prepare us to have Doug in our home as a roommate with a rental lease and with family support and explained to them how much money it would save them. I found out afterwards that someone else did it as well. So, I started opening doors for people to have clients in their homes under a roommate situation with supports from IHSS to pay for staffing because it was less invasive and less restrictive.

It enables it to be a very normal environment. They do it for people who have the elderly stay in their home so why not do it for people living with a disability? There wasn't really a law set, so I don't know why it was so difficult to set up.

We knew we could make it work and it really opened some doors for people that care for an individual to have them in their lives in a normal and safe environment. I wanted it set up so we could do all the things with Doug that he loved without being scrutinised. His health and safety and life were always the priority on my list for Doug, not whether or not I did my dishes and other things that didn't matter like that.

Everybody needs to be treated equally and I never understood why that was so hard when we were bringing Doug into our home. If anybody in our lives invited us somewhere and told us

Doug, Aged 73 (14 February 1948 - 1 August 2021)

Doug couldn't come, then we didn't go. He was treated as an equal family member because that's what he was.

The other thing about having it set up as we did was for Doug to be able to keep learning with self-care and other everyday things around the house. He was always learning right up until the day he passed away. Learning to do more things independently.

It was always important for Doug to be included in everything and it was also important for him to be accountable for poor behaviours and getting rewarded for good behaviour. Just like anybody else, no different.

I had a lot of experience and training in behaviour management and Doug really put me through the cases that's for sure. We were in a restaurant once when Doug made a very inappropriate comment (he did this a lot). If a big person came close to him, he would say, 'Well gee, how do they get their pants over their hip?' And I would turn it around, so it wasn't awkward and I'd ask him, 'Well, how do you get all that crap on your body?'

Everyone would laugh which was great because it would take away the awkwardness and ease the situation. It was always important for Doug to learn what good behaviour was and for others to know he wouldn't get away with it because he had Down syndrome.

Another thing he would say about really tall people was, 'That's a high giant.' I would tell him it was okay because he was able to reach things on the ground because he's short and tall people could reach things high up.

As well as making Doug accountable for his actions and managing his behaviours, I wanted people to see him and understand that he was a person just like them. He didn't deserve to be pushed to the back just because he had Down syndrome.

We went to Disneyland once for an amazing adventure with our friend Uncle Tammy as Doug affectionately referred to her, for his birthday. Mickey and Minnie Mouse were there, and we were waiting to see them with many other families.

Here we were waiting just like everyone else, and all these parents kept pushing their kids in front of Doug. He waited so patiently, and they kept pushing their kids in front of him. It was making me so mad, but I didn't want to cause a scene.

All of a sudden, and I can't remember which character it was now, Mickey or Minnie walked past the kids, took Doug's hand, and went for a walk with him. It was such an amazing moment and I have still have tears in my eyes to this day remembering it. It was such a wonderful moment of inclusion for Doug, and I hope they realise the impact it had.

I'm hoping the parents on that day, saw what happened and realised why it happened. I don't know that they would have, but it was the best example of inclusion and acceptance I have ever seen.

There have been many occasions with Doug where I have said something to people discretely. I've done it that way because I don't want Doug to be affected by the negativity. I hope people realise and change their ways.

Even at home, we would take turns of being first with showers and other things. Everyone likes to be first sometimes, don't

Doug, Aged 73 (14 February 1948 - 1 August 2021)

they? And when Doug would need to go second, we would compromise. You can have a shower second, but you can have dessert first. Taught him it wasn't always important to be first and taught him compromise, while still getting a chance to go first sometimes.

He was an awesome person. When you first meet him, he would come across prim and proper with lots of lovely manners. But he had a real sense of silliness that was fun but could be very annoying at times.

If you gave him the opportunity, he would talk to you for hours, but nobody really knew how to get that out of him. It was quite easy as all you would have to say is tell me about your day, and off he would go.

He didn't enjoy telephone conversations and during Covid there were a lot of those. People would call and ask him a question. One word answer and he would pass the phone to me. I don't think he really understood the concept of the phone and the voice on the other end.

He loved people and would remember everyone. He loved going to church and was very proud of his faith in God. He would get annoyed at me if I didn't feel like going to church. He would tell me it was going to make him cry if we didn't go.

He was a very good friend and I really miss that. He was with me all the time and was there for me as much as I was there for him. He would know if I wasn't feeling right even if I tried to hide it. He would ask me questions, get me a glass of water or a snack just to make me feel good.

He was full of nonsense and jokes and didn't understand when things wouldn't work. I would always make things happen for him, so if something didn't work or work out, he didn't understand and he held me responsible for it.

He didn't want anybody in his stuff and would get angry if you tried. He was a very well-rounded person, loyal, dependable, never called in sick, worked his butt off at the job site and around the house. He had an incredible work ethic and even the night before he passed away, he was outside working at 8pm.

He would call all his family 'his children'. Those are my children, I got children. I don't know how to explain a personality as big as Doug's and give it good justice. He was a big personality in a little body, and he always expected to be treated fairly and included.

He would see everyone equally and if people stared or pointed, I would say 'Hi, I'm Bonnie and this is Doug.' They knew it was a polite way of me asking why they were staring at him. If anybody ever said anything to him, I used to tell them I hope that when they have a child with a disability, they have an instructor like me so I can protect them from people like them. I was very protective of Doug – he was my family.

I would always encourage people to come and talk to him and ask him questions. How do you learn if you don't ask questions? I always hoped it would help people to see him as a person just like they were.

I really miss him. It's not like he grew up and moved out, he grew old and passed away and it has certainly left a big gap in my life. It's hard because I could see the physical progression of

Doug, Aged 73 (14 February 1948 - 1 August 2021)

him getting older, but his mind was always as sharp as a tack. Mentally he never declined.

Some favourite sayings from Doug to make you smile and finish our story …

One time Doug asked me, 'How did father go to heaven without his wallet?'

When I was upset with him, he would say, 'Maybe a hot shower is gonna do it. Make all the bad feelings go down the drain!'

After putting hair gel on Doug's head he says, 'No kidding! Maybe the goop on my head is way gone. Maybe I got a door on my head!'

After redirecting a bad behaviour, he says, 'You better change your mind Bonnie! Maybe God not like it!'

He had a few food items he hated. He would say, 'No I can't eat that. It's not good for my heart.'

From the Hearts of Mums

Afterword

I hope you have enjoyed the stories in this book as much as I have enjoyed meeting with each of these mums, hearing and writing their stories.

At the beginning of the book, I shared that there are common threads besides the fact these families are part of the Down syndrome community.

I wonder if you were able to see that as you read these stories.

For me, the biggest and most wonderful common thread in these stories is the fact that these children are so intuitive with other people's feelings.

The fact they pick up on it and know exactly when someone is not right even when their loved ones are trying to hide it, is such a beautiful quality to have.

Even when you are trying to be strong and not show your family you are hurting, having a hand on your shoulder or a hug out of the blue, really makes your heart swell and begin to feel a little better.

All of these families work very hard with their loved ones to ensure they are able to enjoy the things they love. Extra work as well as therapies helps for this to happen, and even though it can sometimes be hard, they do whatever they can regardless.

We all want the best for our children. We want them to be respected and valued for who they are. They deserve it.

About The Author

Julie Fisher is wife to Mick, Mum to Caleb, Blake and Darcy, Stepmum to Bree and she is also a carer for her son Darcy. Darcy lives with Down syndrome and Julie and her family had to navigate a new world when he joined their family.

After completing her dream of writing her first book *The Unexpected Journey: Embracing the Beauty of Disability* which shares their journey with Darcy, in 2021 she released her second book *The Magic of Inclusion: Give People A Chance and Watch Them Shine* which discusses the importance of inclusion and acceptance as well as how simple it can be. When giving someone a chance, the magic you see is amazing.

Julie has made many connections over the world in the Down syndrome community since writing her books and Darcy has become an Ambassador for Celebrate T21, Making Chromosomes Count, The DS Community News, and he is also an official inclusion warrior for Friend In Me.

Julie has also enjoyed success in working with Carers Victoria, Friend In Me and Down Syndrome Victoria and has recently launched a family support business where she works holistically with families and their children with disabilities.

Following the success of sharing her stories and after hearing many other family's stories, Julie felt it was important to share them. Even though all the stories in this book are about people caring for their children with Down syndrome, you see that they all travel a different path.

Julie continues to see a need to raise awareness around inclusion and acceptance for people with disabilities (and for many others), and part of doing that is by sharing stories from other families.

Her mentors and employers Stuart and Natasa Denman and work colleague Vivienne Mason continue to support Julie in pursuing her dreams of working with families and raising much needed awareness and have been the driving force behind her completing her books.

Julie also speaks regularly to different groups about her caring role as well as inclusion and acceptance in the hope that she can keep spreading the message of awareness for people living with a disability. She can be contacted at her website www.juliefisher.com.au.

About The Author

Julie's hope is for everyone to be treated fairly and the same so they can enjoy life's adventures, and for future families to be given respect and kindness when receiving a diagnosis for their child.

About The Designer

Alexis Schnitger is an artist and mum of three who lives in Brisbane, Queensland. Her eldest son Jordan introduced her to the Down syndrome world, and she has become a fierce advocate, designing the T21 arrow which has been embraced around the globe.

Alexis enjoys reading and is passionate about creating delicious food for family and friends. Her love of art is shared by her three budding artists. They couldn't be happier than when painting with their mum.

Alexis is a visual designer, illustrator and multimedia artist who is currently following her dream and undertaking a bachelor's degree in architecture at QUT (Queensland University of Technology).

With over 15 years' experience in the design industry, Alexis continues to create through freelance design opportunities, as well as within her role of Artistic Director for the social enterprise, Celebrate T21, an organisation that supports people living with Down syndrome and their families.

Alexis illustrated her first children's book in 2022 alongside author Sally Fetouh and she has two more children's books in the works. Stay tuned!

As a fairly recent arrival in Brisbane, when Alexis isn't creating, you will find her and her family exploring everything this incredible city has to offer.

About The Designer

An arrow must be pulled back in order to shoot forward. This is something many of us have felt when hit by an unexpected diagnosis for our child.
This action is preparing us to shoot forward to an amazing future with our incredible kids.

The Roman numerals for 21 are included to represent the 21st chromosome and the dots at either end represent trisomy.

The rings in the centre represent the connections made between families in our community, while the overlapping triangles represent strength and resilience.

Jordy's mum x
Alexis Schnitger

OFFERS

Julie Fisher – Family Support Services

When you have a child with a disability, it can be very challenging working on strategies, goals, support networks and navigating the systems.

If you are unsure where to start and wondering who can assist you, I can work with your family and help you with things you are struggling with. Together, we'll ensure we get the support you and your child need in place.

My family support services can help you with:

- Identifying exactly what you need assistance with
- Understanding what a good support worker looks like

- Completing documentation to access support
- Uncovering strategies for your child to help them be their best
- Planning and reviews to ensure the strategies are working
- Assistance with goal setting, in the short and long term.

Even if it's something you think may be small, the right support can make such a difference.

Get in touch with me to find out more: juliedixie@hotmail.com
Follow Julie Fisher – Family Support Services here:
https://www.facebook.com/JulieFisherFamilySupportServices

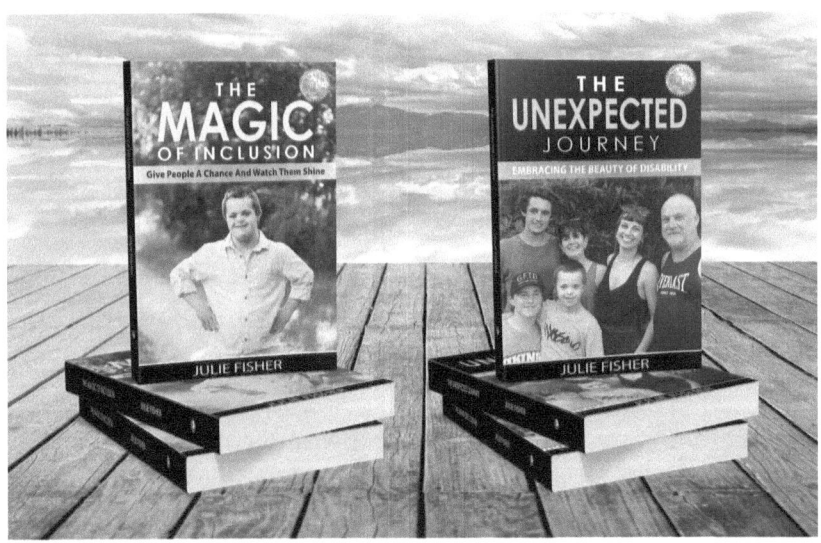

As a mum of a young boy with Down syndrome, Julie Fisher knows firsthand the heartbreak of seeing your child be made to feel like they don't belong. She has also experienced the flipside, where acceptance and inclusion make magic happen, and has made it her passion to educate others on the profound impact even the smallest acts of acceptance and inclusion can have.

Julie's journey began just before the birth of her third son Darcy. When Julie and her family made a decision to provide a life of love, experiences and positivity for Darcy, she was compelled to share their unexpected story. Over the last 17 years Julie's passion for advocating for inclusion and acceptance for all has continued to grow. In making sure Darcy has every opportunity to participate in everything he would like to try, she has watched him thrive - and she is passionate about giving other children and adults of all abilities the chance to do the same.

Now, as the author of three books *The Unexpected Journey*, *The Magic of Inclusion* and *From the Hearts of Mums*, Julie loves speaking to groups of all sizes, in schools, workplaces, support groups and not-for-profits, about the importance of acceptance and inclusion in every aspect of life. She speaks from the heart, in a raw and real way, engaging the audience with her honesty and insights into the world of disability. In promoting awareness of the real and profound impact our actions have on the lives of others, Julie inspires us all to do better.

Julie can speak to your group on a range of topics including:
- The life-changing magic of acceptance and inclusion
- Embracing individuality, diversity and our unique gifts
- Finding the joy in the wonderful world of disability
- Encouraging questions to enrich understanding
- Focusing on abilities and celebrating successes
- Accessing support and making connections
- Providing opportunities and counting every moment
- Creating the experiences and life that everyone deserves

To enquire about speaking opportunities, or to work with Julie, email juliedixie@hotmail.com
Website: www.juliefisher.com.au

Notes

www.ingramcontent.com/pod-product-compliance
Lightning Source LLC
Chambersburg PA
CBHW030254100526
44590CB00012B/402